gourds + fiber

Gourds + Fiber

Embellishing Gourds with Basketry, Weaving, Stitching, Macramé & More

GINGER SUMMIT
JIM WIDESS

An Imprint of Sterling Publishing Co., Inc.
New York

WWW.LARKCRAFTS.COM

EDITOR: **LINDA KOPP**
COPYEDITOR: **JANE LAFERLA**
ART DIRECTOR: **KRISTI PFEFFER**
ILLUSTRATOR: **ORRIN LUNDGREN**
PHOTOGRAPHER: **LYNNE HARTY**
COVER DESIGNER: **CELIA NARANJO**

Library of Congress Cataloging-in-Publication Data

Widess, Jim.
  Gourds + fiber : embellishing gourds with basketry, weaving, stitching, macrame & more / Jim Widess & Ginger Summit. -- 1st ed.
      p. cm.
  Includes index.
  ISBN 978-1-60059-470-0 (pb-trade pbk. : alk. paper)
  1. Gourd craft. 2. Fiberwork. I. Summit, Ginger. II. Title.
  TT873.5.W55 2011
  677'.02832--dc22

                              2010020677

10 9 8 7 6 5 4 3 2 1

First Edition

Published by Lark Crafts
An Imprint of Sterling Publishing Co., Inc.
387 Park Avenue South, New York, NY 10016

Text © 2011, Jim Widess, Ginger Summit
Project photography © 2011, Lark Crafts, an Imprint of Sterling Publishing Co., Inc.,
unless otherwise specified
How-to photography © 2011, Jim Widess
Illustrations © 2011, Lark Crafts, an Imprint of Sterling Publishing Co., Inc.,
unless otherwise specified

Distributed in Canada by Sterling Publishing,
c/o Canadian Manda Group, 165 Dufferin Street
Toronto, Ontario, Canada M6K 3H6

Distributed in the United Kingdom by GMC Distribution Services,
Castle Place, 166 High Street, Lewes, East Sussex, England BN7 1XU

Distributed in Australia by Capricorn Link (Australia) Pty Ltd.,
P.O. Box 704, Windsor, NSW 2756 Australia

If you have questions or comments about this book, please contact:
Lark Crafts
67 Broadway
Asheville, NC 28801
828-253-0467

Manufactured in China

ISBN 13: 978-1-60059-470-0

For information about custom editions, special sales, premium and corporate purchases, please contact Sterling Special Sales Department at 800-805-5489 or specialsales@sterlingpub.com.

For information about desk and examination copies available to college and university professors, requests must be submitted to academic@larkbooks.com. Our complete policy can be found at www.larkcrafts.com.

While this art was born of necessity, it quickly evolved into a more decorative form. Whether you're a weaver or a basket maker wanting to incorporate your art with the beautiful shell of a *Lagenaria siceraria*, or a gourd artist longing to braid, knot, or twine, you'll find you can create exciting works of art by pairing fiber with gourds.

The projects in this book utilize a wide range of materials; some like Pine Needle Perfection (page 51) use traditional fibers like sinew (imitation) and raffia, while others like Long Distance (page 80) experiment with contemporary materials—such as telephone wire—to create an entirely new vision. If you're new to the world of gourd craft, rest assured that the tools are easy to find and use; you may already have all that you need. And finding gourds can be as simple as going to your local farmers' market, doing a quick internet search, or growing your own.

For those of you that have already experienced the joy and satisfaction that comes from working with gourds, you can now take the decorative aspect to a whole different level. Each project features both written instructions and step-by-step photos that will walk you through a variety of fiber techniques that will enhance your gourd-crafting repertoire.

Even though the projects in this book draw from a range of traditional techniques including plaiting and knotting, you'll find they also lend themselves to modern interpretation. Shimmering Net on page 108 illustrates a modern twist by using flexible copper wire to make the netting. In addition to the projects, each chapter features the work of contemporary gourd artists who have used fiber techniques to create beautiful works of art. We encourage you to use their ideas as a source of inspiration for your own work.

CHAPTER 1

GETTING STARTED

A Short History

Grasses and vines, bast from woody shrubs and trees, and animal sinew, hair, and skin were early man's raw fiber materials. Through experimentation, they quickly understood that single strands, whether from plants or animals, had minimal strength. By spinning or twisting multiple strands, they eventually learned to make stronger fiber elements, such as yarn, cordage, and rope, which led to the development of knotting, weaving, and basketry—techniques easily adapted to making gourds more portable.

As our ancestors migrated, they invented and discovered new methods for using fibers to produce handles, bases, tie-downs for lids, and carrying apparatuses for their gourd containers. It was these fiber elements—whether fashioned as belts, cords, straps, thongs, netting, or basket structures—that allowed man to transport gourds overland and by water.

Since form follows function, the embellishment of gourds for the sheer joy of beautification most likely evolved from utilitarian solutions. We know that in many cultures gourds were valued possessions both for the survival of the family as well as for the fortunes of the community. If a gourd suffered the misfortune of a crack or breakage, the damage was carefully repaired, and, in some cases, repaired over and over again. Many times the techniques used for repair, such as lacing and stapling, became the inspiration for decorative embellishment.

Often artisans in a community would take special care to weave, carve, or embellish gourds to make them worthy of royal or special status. Usually these extraordinary artifacts are the ones we find in museum collections around the world. Yet even some of the lowliest gourds used by common folk often had artistically executed embellishments to indicate what the gourd contained.

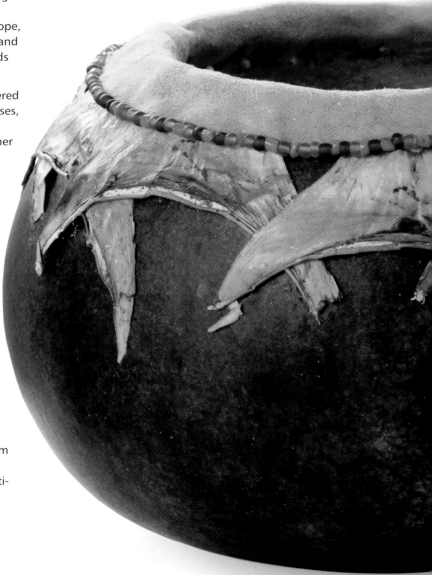

OUT OF AFRICA

Just as human genetic studies have traced the ancestor of all living human beings today to a single mother, geneticists have recently discovered that bottle gourd fragments from the earliest indigenous settlements in the Americas contain genetic evidence of their African origins, yet contain genetic markers linking them to gourds from Asia. This evidence suggests that human beings carried gourds from Africa to Asia and eventually onto the American continent, most likely along the Bering land bridge and the Pacific Coast.

Photo by John Warburton-Lee

A Hamar woman sells fiber-covered gourds at Dimeka, the largest market in the Hamar country of southwest Ethiopia.

Photo by John Warburton-Lee

Kenyan herding family. All of this Turkana family's possessions rest in the gourds hanging in the tree.

Collection of Sue Westhues

An Ethiopian milk gourd is encased in extremely thin leather. The top and bottom are woven with a metal wire embellishment.

An intricate basket structure of cordage weaves up the sides and around the neck of this Indonesian bottle gourd. The hand-carved stopper adds to the drama of this ceremonial container.

STATUS SYMBOL

Many cultures placed a high value on their gourd containers; some families even measured their net worth in the number of gourds they owned. According to Professors Esmé Hennessy and Adrian Koopman at the University of Natal, the royal chiefs were known in Zulu as Amakhosi Oselwa, Chief of the Gourds, attesting to the extreme value the Zulu placed on these fruits.

Betel nuts are kept in this gourd made of woven palm leaves. The tight-fitting lid on the right doubles as a small dish in which the owner places a few pieces, thus protecting his stash from overeager partakers.

This simple antique Japanese ikebana gourd has a wisteria vine for attaching to a peg.

This container from the Philippines was made to hold salt or meat. In tropical climates, gourds have provided a simple means of food storage for tens of thousands of years.

This Yoruban beaded container with removable top probably held sacred objects or medicines.

An example of a phallocrypt, traditionally worn by men of some ethnic groups in New Guinea to cover their genitals. This form of gourd apparel could be a measure of status or purely an adornment.

Old gourd vessel from the Bamum tribe in Cameroon; used for storing palm wine for ceremonies honoring their ancestors. The fetish pieces protect the wine from spirits and persons intending harm.

When the author went to the Jaguar Preserve in Belize, gourd bottles like this one were hanging on the Pepsi machine. The rangers would fill the gourds with either water or Pepsi, and that would be their "water bottle" for the day.

A Japanese farmer's water or sake gourd nestled in a bamboo carrier. Rice farmers in Japan have been carrying their liquids in bamboo woven gourds for centuries.

This drinking gourd was collected from the mouth of the Congo River in 1659. It's covered with an artistic interlacing of palm fiber.

SHAPELY GOURD

There are four basic shapes that help classify gourds:

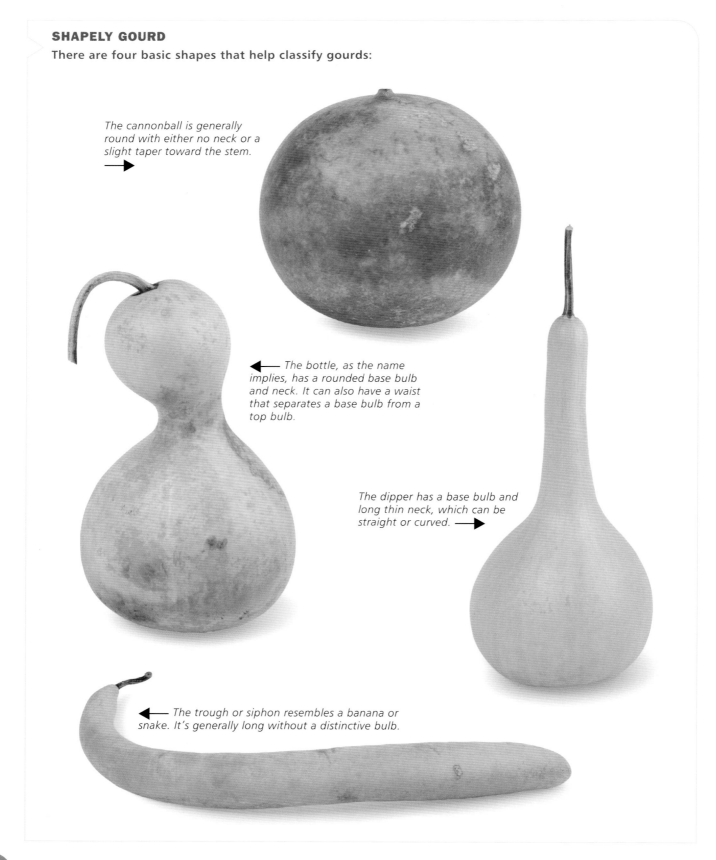

The cannonball is generally round with either no neck or a slight taper toward the stem. →

← *The bottle, as the name implies, has a rounded base bulb and neck. It can also have a waist that separates a base bulb from a top bulb.*

The dipper has a base bulb and long thin neck, which can be straight or curved. →

← *The trough or siphon resembles a banana or snake. It's generally long without a distinctive bulb.*

Selecting and Preparing the Gourd

Each chapter discusses the specific fiber techniques for the projects they contain. However, one constant remains for the projects in the book: They all begin with gourds that have been cleaned, cut or left intact, and finished.

If you've never worked with gourds, the following information will help you select and prepare the gourd so you can begin working the fiber techniques. If you're an experienced gourd crafter, you may want to skim the following material for a quick review.

The projects use the *Lagenaria siceraria* or hardshell variety of gourd. Many gourd artists grow their own, but you can easily find dried gourds at gourd farms and farmers' markets, or through various outlets on the Internet.

CLEANING THE EXTERIOR

Freshly harvested gourds have shells that vary in coloration from ivory to dark green. All the projects, however, begin with cured gourds that have undergone a drying time of anywhere from six weeks to a year after harvest to allow all interior water to leach out of the porous woody shell. The outer epidermis of cured gourds can be creamy tan to dark brown and may have mold on them depending on the method used for drying. You will need to remove the skin and mold to get to the hard shell before cutting the gourd.

There are several ways to clean the exterior. Each involves soaking or moistening the gourd to loosen the skin prior to removal. The most common method is to soak the gourd in a solution of water mixed with a little bleach or disinfectant. Since a dried gourd will float, you'll need to weight it down to keep it submerged. A thick, wet towel will keep the gourd skin wet and also partially submerged.

WASHING MOLDY SKIN FROM THE GOURD SHELL

Soak the gourd from 15 minutes to several hours; then use a plastic or metal scrubbing pad or stiff natural bristle brush to remove the skin. If you notice any blemishes or rough spots, you can use wet/dry sandpaper to remove them, though this is totally optional. Allow the gourd to dry before cutting.

Cured gourds

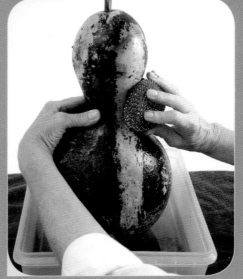

After soaking the gourd can be scrubbed.

CUTTING THE GOURD AND CLEANING THE INTERIOR

You can cut the shell of a dried gourd using hand or power tools. In most cases, using a sharp knife, handsaw, or craft knife will suffice. Avoid using the small round saw blades on motorized rotary craft tools—they're more suited for flat surfaces and will bind or stall when working on the uneven and rounded surface of a gourd. Instead, consider using a small, motorized jigsaw designed for hobby crafters. They work well on most gourds, especially those with thick shells.

Before you cut, use a pencil to draw your cutting line. Place the gourd on a nonskid surface, and use a knife to make a small slit along the line for inserting the saw or knife of choice. Follow the drawn line as you cut through the shell around the gourd.

Open the top of the gourd. Spray a little water into the opening to help keep the dust from becoming airborne. Use your hands to pull out any loose seeds and pulp. Then use a tool to scrape out the remaining pulp. You can devise your own tools; a grapefruit spoon with serrated edge works well. Tools used for sculpting clay or ceramics also work, but you can just as easily improvise with a sharp seashell or other handy kitchen utensil, such as a large serving spoon, ice cream scooper, etc.

Cleaning a dipper gourd presents a different challenge. You will need to find tools that can reach into the narrow neck and down into the bulb. If the opening is wide enough, you can use a long-handled barbecue fork. Otherwise, you can improvise by making tools of sturdy wire, such as a coat hanger.

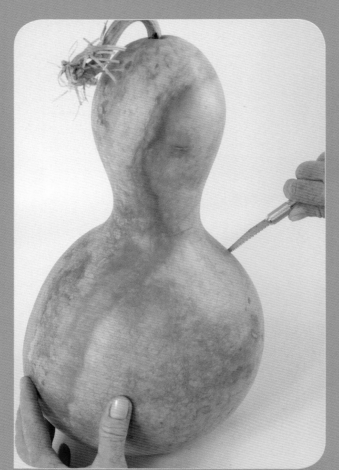

Cutting a gourd using a hobby knife with a #27 saw blade

Cutting a gourd using a mini jigsaw

SAFETY FIRST

The dust from cutting the gourd and from scraping out the seeds and pulp is an allergen to some people. You can avoid any potential problems by always taking a few simple precautions.

Wear a dust mask to prevent inhaling any particles. For maximum protection, you may want to consider using a more elaborate air filtration mask. Don't forget to protect your skin if you're sensitive to dust. Wearing gloves is recommended.

Most gourd crafters prefer to work outside. If you work inside, make sure you are in a room with proper ventilation. Consider using a fan to blow away the dust. You may also periodically stop and use a shop vacuum with a filter to eliminate any dust as you work.

GETTING STARTED

Immersing the open gourd in a tub of water for a week is a very effective means of cleaning the inside of a gourd. After a week, spill out the contents, fill the gourd half full of water, and add sharp gravel. Shake the gourd vigorously and spill out the residue. Rinse, and then allow the gourd to dry for another week.

Use sandpaper or small files to smooth the edges of the opening. Final cleaning and smoothing of the inside of a gourd can be done with a stainless steel pot scouring pad.

Scraping out the gourd's seed mass using a toothed gourd-scraping tool

Using sandpaper to smooth the rough edges of a gourd bowl

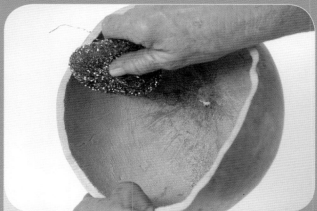

Final cleaning and smoothing of the inside of a gourd can be done with a stainless steel pot scouring pad.

FINISHING THE EXTERIOR AND INTERIOR

Many people consider the natural surface of a gourd beautiful as is. However, the shell is porous, which makes it susceptible to degradation over time. Luckily there are many finishes that will protect and enhance the surface, allowing the gourd's natural beauty to shine through. You will always finish the exterior before you begin working your fiber techniques.

You can paint the surface of a gourd with pigmented paints. If you want a light wash of color, consider using watercolors. If you want a deeper saturation, or wish to create a highly decorated surface, use opaque acrylic or oil paints. Apply watercolors directly to the clean shell, which absorbs some of the paint to give you the washed effect you desire. Varnish the shell first and allow it to dry before applying opaque acrylics or oils. Once you've completed the painting, whether with watercolors, acrylic, or oils, you need to apply a finish to the surface to seal the paint.

If you want more transparency in the coloration, use wood stains, colored inks, or leather dyes. They add interest by allowing the natural mottled pattern of the gourd shell to show through. You can impart a hint of color with one application, or layer them for a deeper, more saturated look. Once you finish a gourd this way, you won't be able to remove the color, since it absorbs into the shell. For best results, test your chosen medium on scraps of shell to determine the effects you like the best.

If you're going to use a fugitive color (one that is prone to fading), first sand the gourd surface using a 180-grit sanding sponge. You'll get much better penetration of the pigment.

Keep in mind that dyes, stains, and inks are more susceptible to fading over time than paints when exposed to light. Using a finish that contains an ultraviolet light shield as a finish coat may help prevent this, though the best precaution is to keep the gourd out of direct sunlight.

Wax and cream shoe polish, either clear or colored, give the shell a subtle sheen. Apply them to the gourd as you would apply polish to a shoe. The longer you leave them on the shell before buffing, the deeper the color. Wax used for floors buffs to a higher sheen than wax used for shoes. For even deeper color penetration and a soft leather-like surface when using wax, apply it, then set the gourd out in the hot summer sun or in a warm oven. Allow it to cool before buffing.

Occasionally a project calls for finishing the interior of a gourd. One of the most common ways is to use black spray paint. You can also use acrylic paint that you apply with a brush.

Applying mahogany shoe wax to the surface of a prepared gourd bowl

Working with Fiber

You might find some fiber terms and techniques foreign to your own craft background. Basket makers, for instance, might not feel entirely comfortable working with the softer yarns and threads for the warps and weft in tapestry weaving or Teneriffe. Or a gourd crafter might not know a spoke from a weaver for some of the projects that incorporate basketry. The advice we give is to go ahead and experiment. You'll find that combining gourds with fiber—and all the different techniques that it involves—is well worth the effort.

SELECTING FIBERS

The projects use both natural and man-made fibers. If you're a basket maker, you'll notice that some projects call for round or flat reed and familiar weaving and twining materials. Even if you've never made baskets, you can easily find all materials at craft supply shops or on internet sites that carry basketry supplies and materials.

Leather strips, twine and cording, artificial sinew, raffia, and yarn are also common materials that are easy to find. A few projects use wire, which most would say stretches the definition of fiber. Nonetheless, you'll find it creates interesting and unique designs.

ATTACHING THE FIBERS

For most of the projects in the book, you attach the fibers directly to the gourd through holes that you drill or punch into the shell. You insert the fibers as directed, then knot the ends or tape them to hold them in place as you begin the technique.

You can use a small, motorized rotary craft tool with a variety of drill bits to drill the holes. Or, you can use a gourd or leather awl, or even a tapestry needle, to pierce the shell. A gourd awl has a straight handle with a long, uniform pointed shaft; a leather awl has a bulb-like handle with a tapered shaft. Each does the job equally well. Before you drill or punch the holes, make sure you mark and measure the position of the holes as directed for more accuracy.

For some projects, you'll attach the fibers to a base cord that circles the gourd. You attach these working strands using a simple lark's head knot. You'll find information on the knots used in this book on pages 122 and 123. Once you've attached the fibers, you're ready to begin. Simply follow the step-by-step process shots to complete each project.

CHAPTER 2

RIMS, HANDLES, BASES, AND LIDS

Though a gourd is a suitable vessel all by itself, adding rims, handles, bases, and lids creates a customized container. These structures allow you to handle the gourd more easily, prevent it from tipping over, and help keep the contents inside where they belong. Though once strictly utilitarian, you'll see they can be artistic as well.

If you're a basket maker as well as a gourd artist, you'll recognize some basic techniques and materials in the projects. Finding materials is as easy as going to a source that carries basketry supplies where you can purchase reed, cane, artificial sinew, and other lacings. Since you need to anchor the materials to the gourd, you'll need to pierce the shell. A small, motorized craft tool with drill bits, or gourd or leather awl, makes this easy to do.

Once you feel comfortable with a technique, you can experiment to find variations on the theme. The gallery photos, showing the work of contemporary gourd artists as well as gourds from different cultures, are meant to inspire your own creative process.

Rims

The rim is the most fragile part of the gourd since it usually receives the most stress, especially if there's no other obvious means for lifting and carrying the piece. The inner portion of the shell is relatively soft and spongy, making the rim susceptible to cracking or crumbling with handling from daily use. Natural materials, such as plant roots, inner bark, plant fibers, leather, or even wire were some of the earliest embellishments used on gourds to reinforce the rims.

The rims on contemporary art gourds usually draw the most focus when they're on display. Artists often decorate the rim alone, or use more elaborate materials for it than they use on the body of the gourd. This serves to extend the dimensions of the gourd, and also to highlight special materials or techniques favored by the artist.

Artist ● Darienne McAuley

Artist ● Sylvia Nelson

Artist ● Flo Hoppe

Handles

Discovering how to add handles to gourds was an important step in their utilitarian development. They can be purely decorative as well as functional. More and more, gourd artists incorporate them into the overall design to enlarge and enhance an art piece.

You can find ready-made handles in craft stores that you can easily attach to a gourd. You can also make them using a wide variety of basketry materials. Just a word of caution: Handles may encourage someone viewing an art gourd to examine it more closely, both inside and out. For this reason, even a decorative handle needs to be strong enough to support the weight of the gourd.

Bases

The easiest base you can make is to mount the gourd on a ring. You can cut rings from gourds, then paint them or wrap them with natural fibers, or leave them as is. You can also purchase metal or rubber rings, or make your own rings by circling leather lacing or cord, or making a ring of wire. Of course you can also purchase ready-made bases in many sizes and styles to complement the gourd.

When you attach fibers to the bottom of a gourd, you can use twining, coiling, or weaving to make a base. Another alternative is to first start a basket, and then as the sides begin to form, insert the gourd. This strategy very neatly solves two dilemmas—keeping the gourd securely upright, and providing a starting point for many basketry techniques.

Lids

Diverse cultures have developed many styles of lids for gourds and techniques for attaching them. Corncobs, bones, and short pieces of wood conveniently fit into the narrow openings of water jugs or carriers. A long bone or stick can act as a lid and dipper, allowing easy access to the contents inside. In China, gourd cricket cages have caps of elaborately carved wood, ivory, or even jade, which provide ventilation and protection for the precious fighting crickets inside.

While artists today have many materials available to them, they frequently opt to use parts of a gourd to make lids and covers that they attach using a hinge, leather, wire, a ring, or loose stitches. Many times a lid may simply be the top portion of the gourd itself.

Another consideration is how to keep the lid from falling into the opening. While many techniques can solve this dilemma, the obvious solution is to cut the lid slightly larger than the opening so that it rests on the rim of the gourd vessel. Another option is to secure a thin strip, or extender, of another material, such as reed or bark, to the vessel so the lid will have something that secures it.

Artist ● Cookie Cala
The handle is lashed through holes in the gourd.

Artist ● contemporary

This treatment strengthens the rim while offering interesting decorative possibilities. You can vary the look by using any material for the lacing.

WHAT YOU NEED

Small **GOURD**, cut in half, cleaned, and finished ● Small, motorized **CRAFT TOOL** with drill bits, or gourd or leather **AWL** ● 30 feet (9.1 m) of #4 **ROUND REED** ● Needle-nose **PLIERS** ● Cyanoacrylate **GLUE** (optional)

WHAT YOU DO

1. Use the craft tool or awl to make holes along the rim of the gourd, approximately ¼ to ⅓ inch (6 mm to 8 mm) from the edge. Space them as evenly as possible, approximately ¾ inch (1.9 cm) apart. The total number of holes needs to be a multiple of five minus two. This small gourd has 38 holes, or 40 minus two.

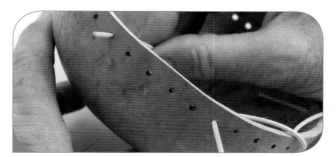

2. Working from inside to outside, anchor the round reed in one of the holes, leaving a 2-inch (5 cm) tail. Count five holes, then thread the reed through the fifth hole from the inside to outside. Repeat threading the reed around the rim of the gourd.

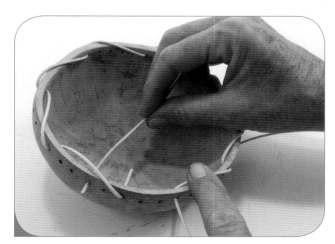

3. When you get back to the starting point, count five holes and insert the reed in the fifth hole, which will be two holes past the beginning point. Continue around the rim until you've filled all the holes.

4. Insert the end of the reed back into the hole you used for the first anchor. This will be a snug fit because it secures the initial anchor and the end piece. Use the needle-nose pliers to pull the ends through.

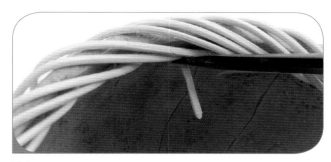

5. You can trim the ends or fold them back into the coiled rim. A touch of cyanoacrylate glue will help to secure the ends as well.

Artist ● Janet Barnett

rims
handles
bases
lids

ROP POINT BEADED RIM DROP POINT BEADED RIM DROP PO
ADED RIM
OP POINT BEADED RIM DROP POINT BEADED RIM DROP POI

DROP POINT BEADED RIM

This lovely rim treatment is deceptively simple yet elegant. You can come up with infinite variations depending on the color of beads you use, the length of the bead strands, and the stringing patterns you choose.

> Designer ● Cindy Lee

WHAT YOU NEED

Small **GOURD**, cut, cleaned, and finished ● 1½ yards (1.3 m) of **ARTIFICIAL SINEW** ● **TAPE MEASURE** ● **PENCIL** ● Small, motorized **CRAFT TOOL** with drill bits, or gourd or leather **AWL** ● Beading **NEEDLE** ● 5 grams of 11/0 seed **BEADS** in matte salmon pink ● 25 grams of 11/0 seed **BEADS** in olive green ● 3 unakite **NUGGETS** ● White **GLUE**

WHAT YOU DO

1. Divide the length of artificial sinew into five strands by gently separating and pulling them apart. Cut each end of each strand on the diagonal for ease of threading.

2. Use the tape measure and pencil to measure and mark around the gourd 1¼ inches (3.2 cm) from the rim. Draw a line parallel to it ¾ inch (1.9 cm) from the rim. Measure the circumference of the gourd at the lower line. Divide this measurement by five, and mark five equidistant points on the line. On the upper line, mark halfway between each of the lower marks. Using the points as your guide, draw the arches.

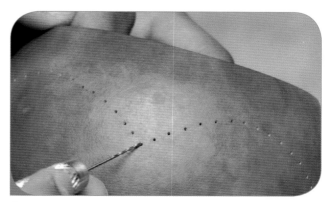

3. Use the craft tool or awl to make holes at each of the lower and upper points. Then, make holes along the arches, spacing the holes approximately ⅛ inch (3 mm) apart. Erase the pencil lines.

4. Thread the beading needle with a strand of sinew. Tie a bead on the end to act as a stopper, leaving a 6-inch (15.2 cm) tail.

GALLERY

Artist ● Kathleen MacIntyre

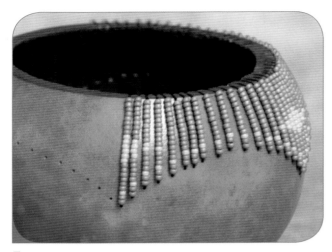

5. Run the threaded needle from the inside of the gourd through one of the five lowest holes. Each strand begins with two green beads followed by one pink bead. When you complete a strand, bring the sinew over the rim and inside the gourd, then come out the next hole in the pattern. Follow the stringing pattern below to make the diamond design.

STRINGING PATTERN

Begin the diamond by starting at one of the lowest holes.

Line 1: two green, one pink, six green, six pink, then green to the rim.

Line 2: two green, one pink, five green, four pink, then green to rim.

Line 3: two green, one pink, four green, two pink, then green to rim.

Line 4: two green, one pink, three green, one pink, then green to rim.

This completes half the diamond. When you reach the third line from the next lowest point, reverse the pattern, working lines 4 to 1, up to the longest line, then repeat the pattern, working lines 2 to 4, to complete the diamond.

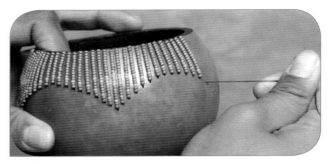

6. Because the beads may not be uniform in size, hold the threaded beads against the gourd now and then to see if you need to add or subtract beads to keep the pattern even. Keep the beaded line snug by pulling the thread straight out from the next hole to avoid cutting the gourd with the sinew.

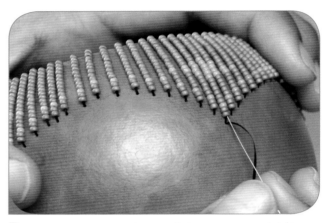

7. Once you've beaded around the entire gourd, bring the sinew through to the front at the bottom of the beaded line. Run the sinew up through the beads and over the rim, and tie the end to the tail you left at the beginning. Spread a coat of the white glue under the strands at the rim to hold the beaded strands in place. Allow to dry.

BEAD CALCULATOR

If you want to change your design, or use a different size gourd, you'll need to alter the amount of beads to use. Here's a simple method for calculating a generous estimate of size 11/0 Japanese seed beads.

There are approximately 16 Japanese seed beads (slightly smaller than other seed beads) per strung inch (2.5 cm). First find the total length of strands, then multiply that number by 16 (beads per inch) to get the total number of beads.

Beads are generally sold by the gram, with about 190 beads per gram. Divide the number of beads by 190 (beads per gram) and you'll get the number of grams of beads you need to buy. Always round the number up, and you'll have more than enough.

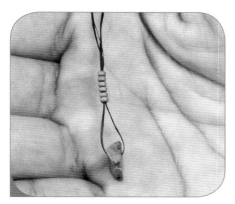

8. String one of the unakite nuggets on a strand of sinew. Make a loop, and string green seed beads on both strands to close the loop. Repeat two times. Make a small hole between the beaded lines near the rim of the gourd. String the strands through the hole to make a cluster, and tie off on the inside of the gourd.

tip ⟶ Artificial sinew is very strong and comes already waxed. It stands up to repetitive stitching and pulling without breaking—a real plus when working with beads.

Artist ● David Snooks

ALNUT SHELL GATHERING BASKET WALNUT SHELL GATHERIN
SKET
THERING BASKET WALNUT SHELL GATHERING BASKET WALN

WALNUT SHELL GATHERING BASKET

By attaching slices of black walnut shells to the sides of a gourd, you can loop round reed around them to anchor the handle. Like many decorative woven handles, you use both a wrapping strand and a pattern strand to achieve the design.

WHAT YOU NEED

Small **GOURD**, cut, cleaned, and finished ● Small, motorized **CRAFT TOOL** with drill bits, or gourd or leather **AWL** ● 2 slices of black walnut **SHELL** ● Tapestry **NEEDLE** ● 30 feet (9.1 m) of waxed linen **THREAD** ● Length of #5 round **REED** that is four times the length of the handle ● **TAPE** or **CLAMPS** ● 100 feet (30.3 m) of 4 mm binder **CANE**

WHAT YOU DO

1. Use the craft tool or awl to make two to four holes in each side of the gourd. Attach the slices of black walnut, one to each side, using the tapestry needle and waxed linen thread. Use a piece of the round reed as a spacer when you stitch to leave a space between the slice and the shell.

2. Wrap the round reed between the slice and the shell on both sides of the gourd, leaving enough length for a suitable handle. Cut the length of round reed to end approximately at the walnut shells. Use the tape, clamps, or ends of thread to temporarily secure the ends.

3. Cut a length of the 4 mm binder cane longer than the handle length, and insert it under the wrapping strand but on top of the reed. Wrap the binder cane around the entire handle including the end of the binder cane for approximately 1 inch (2.5 cm) before beginning the decorative pattern.

4. Wrap around the handle but under the binder cane strip. Continue in this manner, with every other wrap going under the middle reed, until you near the end of the handle on the other side. Wrap all elements together, bury the end of the binder cane back up into the handle, and pull tight.

HISTORIC HANDLES

This method allows you to attach a handle without putting any holes in the gourd. As you study utilitarian gourds from around the world, you'll discover that the vast majority of them have handles fashioned in this way.

Here's the basic formula: Fashion two rings from a fibrous material. Place one above and one below the widest circumference of the gourd. Attach the handles to the top ring. Lash the two rings together while holding them in position. Take care to keep both rings parallel to each other and horizontal on the gourd.

A Western Apache water gourd collected in the 1940s has a corncob stopper. The woven vine, probably Chusquea coronalis, provided a support for a carrying handle.

The woven base allows this top-heavy bohka Indonesian water gourd to sit upright in a canoe. The lashing to the upper ring holds the base in place.

Collection of Sue Westhues

Artist ● Patricia Berry
A driftwood handle is stitched to a bull kelp lashed rim.

This tall bottle from SE Asia would never have stood up by itself.

HANDLES

28   WALNUT SHELL GATHERING BASKET

SWING-HANDLE BASKET

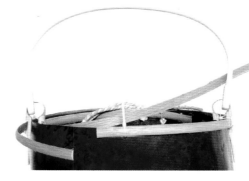

Artist Susie Billingsley shows how you can attach a purchased swing handle to a gourd, much as you would attach it to a basket.

A replica of a water carrier used by Dayak children in Borneo. A simple ring passes through two holes in the top of the gourd; the holes serve for both filling and dispensing water. The gourd is easy to carry and the water doesn't slosh out, making it a perfect vessel for a child's chore.

A swing handle connects to the rim of the gourd with two loops known as ears. Each ear has a notch that locks into the rim when you drive a decorative rivet through the ear and into the gourd. The rim consists of two lengths of flat oval or split round reed.

Artist ● Jennifer Wool
A square rattan teapot handle is attached to the gourd through holes drilled in the rim of the gourd. The body of the gourd is woven with rattan peel and cane.

Susie fit the two pieces for the rim to the inside and outside of the gourd by slipping the reed into the notches on the ears. Using holes she drilled around the rim of the gourd, Susie lashed the reed in place. To finish the gourd, she hung ornamental cords from each of the ear rivets.

TWINED BASE

Adding stability to a gourd is as easy as making a simple twined base. Once completed, you can use it as the starting point for other basketry techniques. This is the base for Rippled Rim in chapter 7.

WHAT YOU NEED

GOURD, cut, cleaned, and finished ● **COMPASS PENCIL** ● Small, motorized **CRAFT TOOL** with drill bits, or gourd or leather **AWL** ● 20 yards (18 m) of leather **LACING** ● **LACING TOOL** ● Round-nose **PLIERS**

WHAT YOU DO

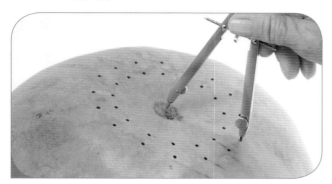

1. Use the compass on the bottom of the gourd to lay out two concentric circles that are approximately 1 inch (2.5 cm) apart. Use the pencil to mark holes on the outer circle that are approximately ⅜ inch (9.5 mm) apart. Then mark corresponding holes on the inside circle. Use the craft tool or awl to make the holes.

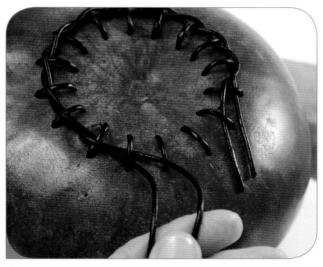

2. Thread the leather lacing from the inside through two holes to make a vertical stitch. Continue around until you've filled all the holes. Do not tie off the ends. Insert two lengths of lacing in corresponding holes and twine around the base for several courses.

3. Continue twining around until you've filled the space between the vertical stitches. When you finish, use the lacing tool to hide the ends of the strands under the weave.

4. Use the round-nose pliers to tighten the lacing stitches you made in step 3. When you finish, secure them by tying the two ends together on the inside of the gourd.

Artist ● **Betty Herrington**

Artist ● **Marla Helton**

Artist ● **traditional**
Woven palm serves both decorative and utilitarian purposes on this palm-wine bottle from Senegal.

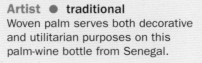

BASES

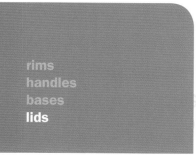

Adding extenders to a gourd creates a snug-fitting lid. You can use various materials for the extenders, but flexible bark, such as cedar, works particularly well for this design.

WHAT YOU NEED

GOURD, cut in half, cleaned, and finished ● Small, motorized **CRAFT TOOL** with sanding tip and drill bits ● White **GLUE** or carpenter's glue ● Cedar **BARK**, 2½ times the diameter of the gourd in length ● Gourd or leather **AWL** ● Tapestry **NEEDLE** ● Waxed linen **THREAD** ● Strip of **LEATHER**, twice the diameter of the gourd in length (*optional*) ● Strip of **FABRIC**, the diameter of the gourd in length ● **CLOTHESPINS**

WHAT YOU DO

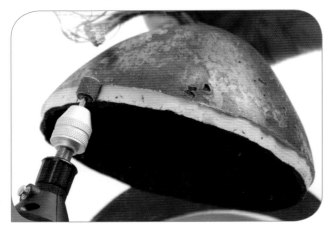

1. Cut the gourd in half. Because you want the bark extender to be vertical when you attach it, use the drill with the sanding tip to sand the outer edge of the top of the gourd (the lid) to make a lip.

2. Apply the glue to the lip, and attach the extender. Use the craft tool or awl to make evenly spaced holes, one on top of the other, through the shell and extender all the way around. Use the tapestry needle and waxed linen to stitch the extender to the lid. If desired, add a strip of leather to cover the join as you stitch.

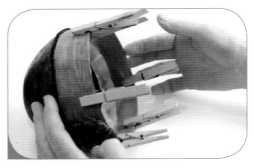

3. Glue the strip of fabric on the inside of the lid to further reinforce the extender. Make sure the fabric strip straddles the join. Use the clothespins to hold the fabric in place while the glue dries.

4. For the bottom of the gourd, sand the edge as you did in step 1 except this time sand the inner shell. This allows the extenders to overlap. Glue the bark to the shell, and stitch as you did in step 2. If desired, add a strip of leather to cover the join as you stitch. You won't need to glue a fabric strip on the inside.

5. Since the top extender had some outer bark left on it, I decided to leave it and use it as a design element. To finish the gourd, I added a wood-burned design as a complement to the bark pattern.

BUTTONED UP

Very often in Africa you'll find gourds covered with leather to protect them from becoming cracked with use. This also provides a unique way for attaching a lid. After stitching or lacing the leather in place to fit the contour of the gourd, extend the lacing to attach the lid. Then fashion a small loop from leather or thread, and sew it to the lid. Finally, attach a small button or hook to the lacing around the rim opposite the loop.

HINGED LID

If your gourd is thick enough, you can use tiny wood screws to attach a hinge to the shell. Artist Marjorie Albright demonstrates this technique in this lidded gourd. After cutting straight across the gourd to make the lid, she held it in place with a wide hinge and a secure latch.

Artist ● **Marjorie Albright**

Artist ● **Art & Diane Mate**
By cutting 4 inches (10.2 cm) from the top of the gourd, the maker created both a dipper and stopper. A strip of leather lacing attaches the lid to the vessel.

Artist ● **traditional**
These three nesting gourd boxes are from Mali.

CHAPTER 3

LACING, COUCHING, AND STAPLING

Most cultures employ a variety of techniques for repairing gourds that have been cracked or chipped. Many museums throughout the world showcase such gourds. Today, artists often use the same utilitarian techniques—lacing, couching, and stapling—to turn a gourd into an artistic masterpiece.

Lacing brings two or more edges of a material together. Couching is a technique that attaches items to the surface of the gourd, such as leather strips or natural materials, using either plain or fancy stitching. Stapling gets its name because the technique inserts the ends of a short piece of stiff material into two drilled holes, much akin to the modern concept of stapling.

Even though you may have little need to repair a gourd, these techniques, born of necessity long ago, offer you the means to create new and exciting designs. Whether you use natural materials or contemporary fibers, you'll find the potential for developing new forms almost limitless.

Lacing

It's difficult to even speculate the beginning uses and forms of lacing on gourds. Very early on, man used strips of lacing to hold or carry gourds and eventually understood how to employ sewing techniques for repairing a gourd. Most likely the original materials for lacing were vines, grasses, leather, and sinew, much the same materials people used for sewing when making an article of clothing.

GALLERY

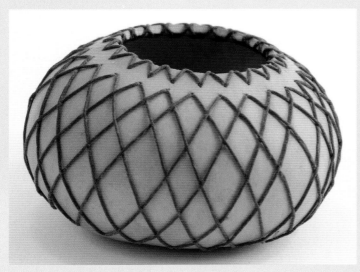

Artist ● David Blackwell

Artist ● Carola Farthing
Gourd seeds used as decoration

Cultures separated by great distances and time surprisingly share consistent lacing patterns. Not only are the patterns utilitarian, but can be decorative as well. As on other objects, lacing on gourds can decorate a rim, outline a pattern, or simply provide visual and textural design elements.

Couching

Couching, a variation of lacing, is where an artisan secures thread, cord, or natural materials to the surface of the gourd. Most likely it was initially used as a way to hide a crack. For purely decorative purposes, the stitching doesn't limit you to following the line of a crack, but allows you to secure materials using fancy lacing patterns of any shape and length.

Use chalk to draw a line along the intended path of your design. Then drill holes along the line that are only wide enough for the needle and cord to pass through. If you are attaching a wide material, such as a bunch of pine needles, drill a double line of holes. The extra stitching the added holes allow will ensure the materials lie flat on the surface of the gourd. When you want to feature the texture and colors of the applied material instead of the stitching, you only need to use a simple overhand stitch to secure it.

Stapling

This technique serves to hold two edges together when repairing a cracked gourd. To work this technique, you drill two small holes in the surface of the gourd, and then insert the ends of a stiff material into each hole. Lining up several of these staples reinforces the repair, or you can create intricate patterns for a purely decorative effect. While each staple needs to be relatively short and straight, you can combine them to make circles, triangles, and curved paths on the gourd's surface.

Artisans in different parts of the world use various materials for this technique. North American Indians use both dyed pine needles and split porcupine quills. The Zulu tribe of southern Africa often decorates small gourds for snuff containers using different colors of metal, such as brass, copper, and tin. They then often rub pitch over the design to help fix the wire to the gourd.

Artist ● Jean Jones
The shape of the *Devil's Claws* dictated the form of each dancer. The heads are scavenged rings or circles of gourd.

Artist ● traditional
A thin, dyed, split vine was used for the embellishments on this gourd from Togo.

CRAZY QUILT GOURD CRAZY QUILT GOURD CRAZY QUILT GO
UILT GOURD **CRAZY QUILT GOURD** CRAZY QUILT GOURD C
OURD CRAZY QUILT GOURD CRAZY QUILT GOURD CRAZY

CRAZY QUILT GOURD

Any quilt artist knows the lure of adding decorative stitches to a pieced design. For this project, you can embellish the individual shards with patterns based on fancy stitches before lacing the gourd back together.

WHAT YOU NEED

GOURD, cleaned, and finished ● **PENCIL** ● Small, motorized **CRAFT TOOL** with drill bits, or gourd or leather **AWL** ● **CRAFT KNIFE** or motorized jigsaw ● Leather **LACING** ● Decorative copper or beaded **TACKS** and **BRADS** (optional) ● Paste **WAX**

WHAT YOU DO

1. Draw the cutting lines on the gourd. Use the craft tool or awl to make holes for the lacing along the cutting lines; do this when the gourd is whole. Make sure each hole has a matching hole on the other side of the line. Use the craft knife or motorized jigsaw to cut the gourd apart.

GALLERY

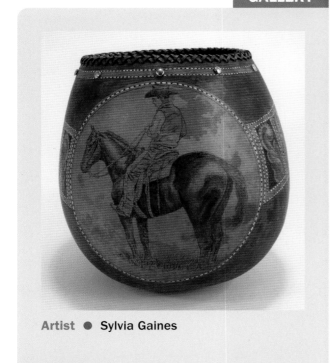

Artist ● Sylvia Gaines

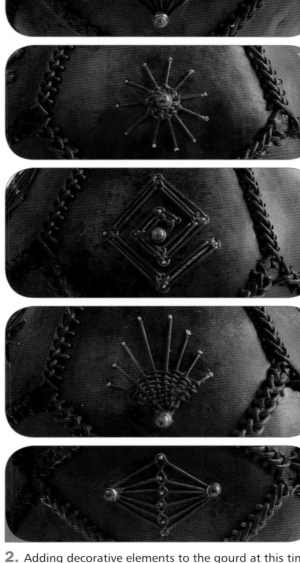

2. Adding decorative elements to the gourd at this time is optional. You make the designs using the decorative tacks and brads and the lacing. You can simply wrap the lacing around the tacks and brads, or incorporate weaving or twining techniques for more intricate designs. Use the patterns as shown, or create your own.

LACING

3. Assemble the gourd beginning with the bottom. The easiest lacing pattern is an X made from back-and-forth diagonal stitches.

4. For a different lacing pattern, complete the first X. Then insert the lacing through the next lower hole, and bring the end under the one above where the lacings cross. Pull tight, take the lacing down to the next hole, and continue in this way until you complete the section.

5. To finish, apply a coat of the paste wax to fill any edges on the holes.

tip ➤ You can vary the lacing pattern on each cut section or keep the pattern consistent throughout.

Variation

Artist ● **Ginger Summit**
Here is a variation cut into six sections before lacing it together. Observe how the lacing adds a new dimension to what was simply a smooth bottle.

Artist ● **Harold Sampson**

REPAIRS AROUND THE WORLD

Cultures from opposite sides of the earth use similar lacing techniques to repair gourds. Through them, you can see how lacing, couching, and stapling developed.

Hawaiians most commonly repaired gourds using native fibers. They drilled holes on either side of the crack, then stitched from side to side along the length of the break, and then back again, to create a wedge-shaped pattern. Sometimes they filled the drilled holes with a pitch to make the vessel stronger or waterproof. The pitch they used was probably a mixture of the gum of a tree mixed with pumice or soil.

In Africa, gourds are so valuable they're always mended rather than discarded. Today, Africans still repair gourds in a very similar way to the Hawaiians by drilling holes along the edges of the crack and stitching through them. However, they first apply a pitch or glue to the edges of the crack. Then they use a simple lacing pattern that creates a braid-like design over the crack.

A challenge arose when repairing a gourd with a narrow neck, which prohibits stitching. In this case, they glued the crack with pitch, and then covered it with a braid or rows of cord—a possible precursor to decorative couching. Eventually they learned they could secure the crack with thin metal strips—staples—which they coated with additional pitch to keep them in place.

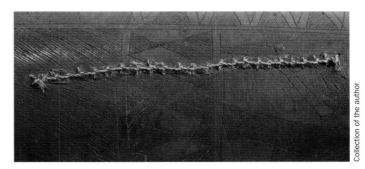

Sewn repair on a Masai milk gourd.

Copper wire lacing was used to repair the cracks in the gourd body of this African water pipe.

Detail: Copper wire is used to lace a crack back together on this African water pipe.

Metal staples mended this Kenyan example. A tool worked through the mouth of the gourd bent the prongs of the staples to close them, then a length of cordage was glued on top of the staples to hide them.

LACING

lacing
couching
stapling

DRAMATIC *DRACAENEA DRACO*

Long a favorite material of basket makers, the orange to dark brown shading
of dried *Dracaenea draco* provides a dramatic contrast to a gourd's stained shell.
By soaking the leaves, you can shape them to the contour of any gourd.

WHAT YOU NEED

GOURD, cut, cleaned, and finished ● Small, motorized CRAFT TOOL with drill bits, or gourd or leather AWL ●
DRACAENEA DRACO LEAVES, enough to encircle the rim of the gourd ● Tapestry NEEDLE ● Waxed linen
THREAD ● SCISSORS ● White GLUE ● Clear PLASTIC WRAP ● TAPE ● #4 round REED

WHAT YOU DO

1. Soak the *Dracenea draco* leaves until they're flexible. Meanwhile, use the craft tool or awl to make the holes approximately 1 inch (2.5 cm) from the rim.

2. Evenly space and overlap five leaves. With the tapestry needle and waxed linen thread, stitch through and around the fifth leaf, leaving the others unattached for a later step.

3. Add and stitch several more leaves. Cut off the long ends of the first leaves to reduce bulk. Continue adding, stitching, and cutting until the leaves encircle the rim. Do not discard the ends.

4. Cut the ends off the last leaves. Lift the first four leaves you didn't stitch, and tuck the last leaves underneath before stitching them in place. Gently ease the leaves, shaping them to please the eye and to complement the shape of the gourd.

5. Apply the white glue between each leaf and end, as well as between the leaves and the shell.

6. Hold the leaves in place while the glue dries by wrapping the gourd with plastic wrap secured with tape. Cut a hole through the plastic wrap in the center of the gourd to allow moisture to escape. Let the glue to dry thoroughly before cutting off the wrapping.

7. Twine an extended rim. First, drill or punch holes through the gourd and leaves for the #4 round reed. Insert pieces of reed to act as spokes, looping the pieces up through adjacent holes. For more on twining, see chapter 5.

8. Use the ends you trimmed from the leaves to twine around the reed spokes until the weaving reaches your desired length.

Variation

Artist ● **Cookie Hanson**

FOR EMPHASIS

Artist Joy Zuehls shows how couching can add decorative emphasis to a gourd.

First, Joy cut the rim of the gourd along an interesting curved line. She then drilled holes approximately 1 inch (2.5 cm) apart along a line parallel to the cut and at a suitable distance that would emphasize the color contrast.

After painting and coloring the gourd, she formed the ropes into the desired shape and glued the ends together for a clean fit. After wrapping the rope, she stitched it to the gourd through the holes using with the same yarn she used for wrapping.

Designer ● Joy Zuehls

GALLERY

Artist ● Art Lowy

Artist ● Gloria Small

Artist ● Linda Pietz

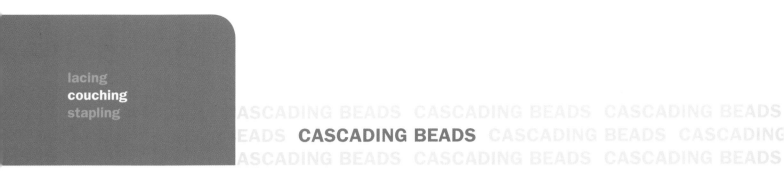

CASCADING BEADS   CASCADING BEADS   CASCADING BEADS
EADS   CASCADING BEADS   CASCADING
ASCADING BEADS   CASCADING BEADS   CASCADING BEADS

CASCADING BEADS

Attaching beads or buttons to a gourd is similar to couching, except you attach each piece with individual stitches rather than stitching over a continuous length of material. It's a great way to use the wonderful variety of buttons and beads available today.

WHAT YOU NEED

GOURD, cut, cleaned, and finished ● Small, motorized **CRAFT TOOL** with drill bits, or gourd or leather **AWL** ● Flat disc **BEADS** in various sizes and colors ● Beading **NEEDLE** ● Invisible beading **THREAD** ● Spray **VARNISH**

WHAT YOU DO

Stitch the beads on the gourd using the beading needle and strong, invisible beading thread. Place the smallest beads along the neck of the gourd, and gradually vary both the size and color of the beads to cover the entire surface. Once all the beads are in place, apply spray varnish to enhance the colors of the beads.

BEAUTIFUL BUTTONS

Artist ● Ginger Summit

The button blankets made by the Haida Indians of the Pacific Northwest inspired the design for this gourd. Europeans introduced the pearl white buttons to the culture, and the Indians quickly added them to blankets they used for dancing. Traditionally, they separated the colors black and red by a row of buttons. They also used additional buttons to make images, such as bear, eagle, raven, or whale, for the blanket interiors.

GALLERY

Artist ● Kathleen MacIntyre

This wire technique, borrowed from the Zulu, features a geometric pattern; you can also create curvilinear forms depending on the placement of the holes. You should always sketch your designs before transferring them to the gourd.

WHAT YOU NEED

GOURD, cut, cleaned, and finished ● **PENCIL** ● Gourd or leather **AWL** ● Wire **CUTTERS** ● 20 inches (50.8 cm) of 18-gauge silver, copper, or brass **WIRE** ● Needle-nose **PLIERS** ● Basketry **PACKING TOOL** or table **KNIFE** ● Roofing **TAR**

WHAT YOU DO

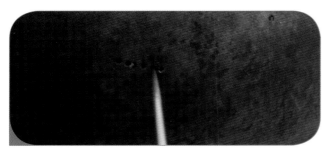

1. Sketch the pattern to see how the wires will lie against each other. Transfer the design to the gourd. Use the awl to make the holes. Position the holes close together, but leave sufficient shell between them.

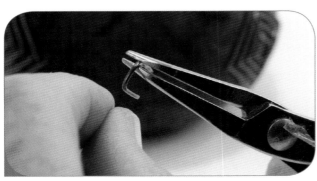

2. Determine how long each piece of wire needs to be to span the holes, then add 2 inches (5 cm) to that length. Use the wire cutters to cut the wire to length. Use the needle-nose pliers to bend a right-angle on each end of the wire piece to make 1-inch (2.5 cm) prongs.

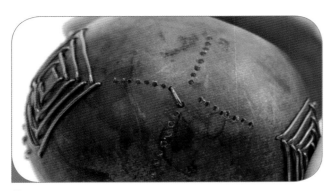

3. Insert the prongs into two holes.

4. Use the packing tool or the end of a table knife to push the wire flat against the gourd shell.

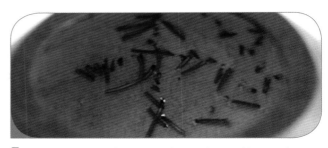

5. On the inside of the gourd, use the packing tool or table knife to bend the wire prongs against the shell.

6. To prevent the wire from lifting from the gourd's surface, and to give the gourd an aged appearance, smear a small amount of roofing tar over the whole gourd, then wipe it off.

Artist ● traditional
Zulu wired gourds

STAPLING

49

CHAPTER 4

COILING

Coiling is perhaps the most popular basketry technique employed by gourd artists because they can easily adapt it for making rims, lids, bases, and an endless array of decorative embellishments. There are two main elements in this technique: The foundation, or the material that makes the coil; and the stitching, which attaches the coils to each other to build the structure.

The material you use for the foundation determines the rigidity of the structure. You can use many materials as long as they are moderately flexible, including all types of natural fibers, cords, and even wire. There's an even greater choice of materials you can use for stitching. Any flexible material can work as long as it's able to withstand the tension and abrasion of repetitive stitching. Natural materials such as raffia, threads, cords, and leather strips work well. You can even use ribbons and wire.

Just as there's a wide variety of materials available for coiling, there's a variety of coiling techniques and stitches that cultures around the world have used over the ages.

The range of coiling styles artists use today reflect this international influence, as you will see in the gallery photos.

Coiling Techniques

The following projects use pine needles, rope, and leather lacing for their foundation materials. Pine needles are a favorite with basket makers and gourd artists because they coil well and are easy to stitch together. You can easily add more needles to keep the coil a consistent diameter.

The split stitch—bringing the needle through the strands of a stitch to split it—is the basis for other stitches you can use when coiling. Each creates its own pattern. Before you begin a project, select a stitch that will complement the overall design of your gourd. You may want to make a sampler gourd using each stitch as you learn the techniques.

Once you master the basics of coiling, you'll want to experiment to create different effects. Then you can go on to add beads, shells, or natural objects for even more embellishment options.

GALLERY

Artist ● Kay van Hoesen

Artist ● Darienne McAuley

Artist ● Keely LeBlanc

PINE NEEDLE PERFECTION

Use the simple split stitch to attach your coils or try some of the stitch variations to enhance your design. A coil gauge, which you can make from metal tubing or even a drinking straw, keeps the coil a uniform diameter to give you perfect results the first time around.

> Designer ● Linda Pietz

WHAT YOU NEED

GOURD, cut, cleaned, and finished ● **PINE NEEDLES** ● **TAPE MEASURE** ● **PENCIL** ● Small, motorized **CRAFT TOOL** with drill bits, or gourd or leather **AWL** ● #18 tapestry **NEEDLE** ● **RAFFIA** or imitation sinew ● **SCISSORS** ● **COIL** gauge cut from copper or brass **TUBING** or a drinking straw

WHAT YOU DO

1. Prepare the needles by soaking them in hot water for 30 minutes. Pick off the caps (the sheaths). Note: *Pinus palustris* has three needles in each bundle; other species of pine have anywhere from two to five needles in a bundle.

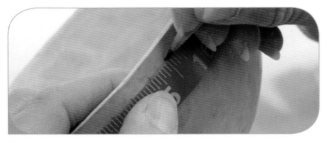

2. Use the tape measure and pencil to mark points ¼ inch (6 mm) from the rim, then draw a line around the rim connecting the points. Mark points on the line ³⁄₈ inch (9.5 mm) apart and evenly spaced. Use the craft tool or awl to make the holes at these points.

3. Determine which sides of the gourd will be the front and back. You'll start the first row, known as the couching row, at the back. The coil is thinner when you first attach it, and then gradually expands to its full diameter. The coils on the back will be angled while the coils on the front will be horizontal.

4. Thread the tapestry needle with 7 to 8 feet (2.1 to 2.4 m) of raffia or sinew. Pass the needle through one hole in the gourd from outside to inside, leaving a 2-inch (5 cm) tail. Bring the needle back out the adjacent hole to the right.

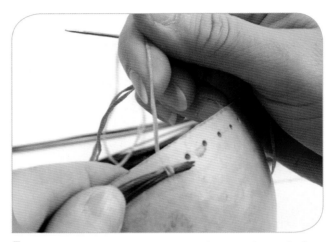

5. Make a bundle of two pine needles. Lay the end of the bundle at the edge of the next hole to the right of where the thread emerged and on top of the sinew. Insert the needle back into the same hole from which it emerged. Pull the needle and thread tight around the bundle of needles.

6. Bring the sewing needle out the adjacent hole to the left. Loop the sinew over the bundle of needles, and then insert needle back into the same hole.

7. Add needles to fill the bundle, being careful to keep all of the individual needles aligned, straight, and parallel. Continue tucking one needle into the center of the bundle before each of the next three stitches. Draw the sinew tight around the bundle as you progress to the adjacent holes to the left.

9. Line up the needles to be straight and parallel. Add one needle at a time, sheath end first, to the center of the bundle. Push the needle into the bundle only as far as necessary to hold it in place. Remember to continue adding needles to the coil as the gauge loosens. Note: Keeping the gauge close to the stitch gives you more control over the pine needles.

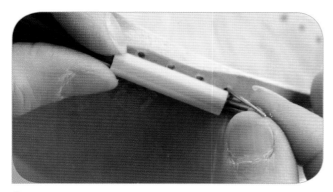

8. When the diameter of your bundle approaches the diameter of the gauge, it's time to carefully slip the gauge around the pine needles. Slide the gauge all the way to the hole for the next stitch.

10. To add a new length of sinew, bring the needle back around and underneath the coil to the outside through the hole of the last. Pull the sinew tight, and cut it, leaving a 2-inch (5 cm) tail. Thread the needle with a new length, and split the stitch through the middle of the stitch and through the center of the same coil where the tail of the old sinew is hanging. Pull the needle completely through the stitch to the inside of the gourd.

GAUGING PERFECTION

The gauge controls the pine needles in three ways: It controls the size of the coil, it lets you know when you need to add more pine needles, and it keeps the needles in alignment. Think of it this way— without the gauge, your bundle will look like it's having a bad hair day.

There's no set rule for adding needles to the gauge. The gauge loosens as you stitch coils. Because the needles vary in length and thickness, sometimes you add a new needle every stitch, sometimes every second or third stitch.

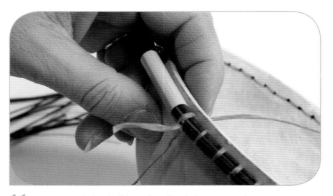

11. Leave a 2-inch (5 cm) tail of the new sinew on the outside of the gourd. Take another stitch over this same stitch to cover it up, then give the sinew a tug, and continue.

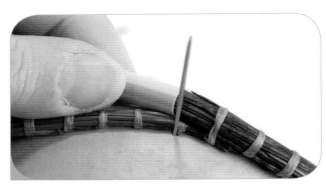

12. When you get back to your first stitch, you've completed the couching row. The next row begins the first actual row of coiling. Because the beginning of the couching row is thinner than the rest of the row, overlap it with the coil and take the first three stitches of the new row.

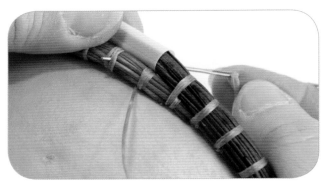

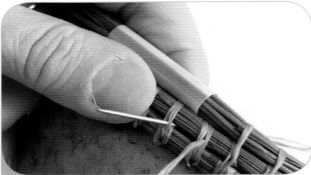

13. After taking the third stitch, begin the split stitch. Bring the sinew out of the hole and up around both coils. Angle the needle through the upper part of the lower coil to split the stitch, coming through the middle of the first coil to the outside of the gourd. Each successive stitch on this row will split the stitch in the previous row.

Stitch Variations

You can complete the coiling using only the split stitch, or you can work the following variations to complete the coiling as a stitch sampler.

WHEAT STITCH

The wheat stitch is made of two stitches, a vertical stitch and a diagonal stitch. To make it, first split the stitch in the previous row and bring the sinew straight up and around the coil to make the vertical stitch. Then bring the sinew back through the same stitch in the previous row, and angle it diagonally to the left to make the diagonal stitch. Split the next stitch in the previous row and repeat around the coil.

VERTICAL WHEAT STITCH

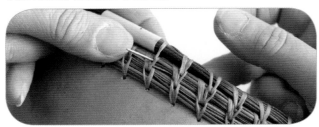

Both stitches of the wheat stitch split only the vertical stitch in the wheat stitch on the previous row.

DIAGONAL WHEAT STITCH

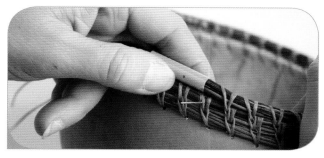

You make the diagonal wheat stitch much like the vertical wheat stitch, except both stitches of the wheat stitch split only the diagonal stitch in the wheat stitch on the previous row.

FERN STITCH

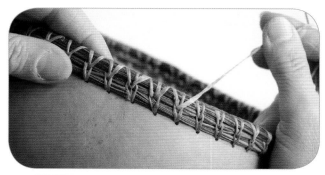

First work a row of the wheat stitch to the left. When the row is complete, stitch the row again, taking a diagonal stitch to the right of each vertical stitch of the wheat stitch. You start to see the beauty of the stitch after the third row.

DIAMOND STITCH

Begin with a previous row of split stitches. First, you make a split stitch moving to the left around the rim. When you complete the row, you reverse directions to take a stitch diagonally to the right around the same row. This makes a V between each stitch. On the next row, you take a stitch between the Vs, sewing to the left. When you complete the row, you reverse direction to make a stitch to the right around the same row.

CHECKERBOARD STITCH

This stitch wraps the sewing element around the foundation several times between every other split stitch to create the checkerboard effect. On each successive row, wrap the coils that fall in between the wrapped coils of the previous row. You'll need to work at least three to five rows before you clearly see the effect.

FREE-FLOATING COIL

A free-floating coil provides an easy way to bridge a gap in a curved rim or cutout gourd. It's the perfect design element for adding interesting negative space to your project.

> Designer ● Linda Pietz

WHAT YOU NEED

GOURD, cut with a curved rim or side cutout, cleaned, and finished ● PINE NEEDLES ● Small, motorized CRAFT TOOL with drill bits, or gourd or leather AWL ● RAFFIA or imitation sinew ● SCISSORS ● #18 tapestry NEEDLE ● COIL gauge cut from copper or brass tubing or a drinking STRAW

WHAT YOU DO

1. Prepare the needles by soaking them. Use the craft tool or awl to make holes along the curve. Begin your coiling, and continue adding needles to the gauge as you move it with each stitch.

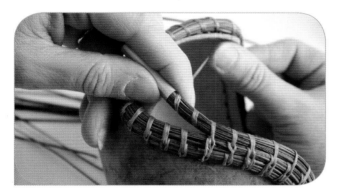

2. When you reach the place where you're going to begin the free-floating coil, use the gauge to extend the coil to the desired length by wrapping the raffia or sinew around the coil using the same spacing as the stitching. Be careful not to torque or twist the needles as you extend the coil.

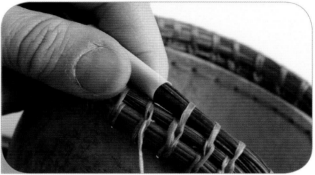

4. Pull the stitch snug, keeping the gauge right next to the stitch. If you allow the gauge to slip down the coil, the needles begin to balloon and lose their parallel alignment, as shown in the photo above, top. If you keep the gauge next to the stitch, it helps control the needles, as shown in the photo directly above.

3. Place the wrapped coil on the opposite side of the gap to find a suitable docking point. Insert the tapestry needle from the back through the middle of the next stitch on the previous coil to split the stitch. Pull the needle and sinew through the stitch.

Artist ● Sue Yamins

Add creative color components by wrapping the foundation element with yarn as you coil. This ancient technique immediately expands your design dynamics.

WHAT YOU NEED

GOURD, cut, cleaned, and finished ● Craft PAPER ● PENCIL ● Craft DRILL, or gourd or leather AWL ● FIBER RUSH or JUTE ROPE approximately the same thickness as the gourd shell ● YARN in miscellaneous colors ● Masking TAPE ● Tapestry NEEDLE

WHAT YOU DO

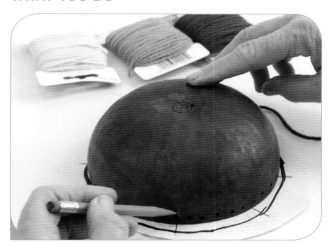

1. Place the gourd on the craft paper and trace around it. Mark evenly spaced points on the traced line, spacing them approximately as far apart as the width of your finger. Transfer the marks to the gourd, and use the craft tool or awl to make holes around its rim.

2. Gather one end of the foundation material and one end of each of the different colored yarns into a bundle. Wrap the bundle with masking tape for approximately 1½ inches (3.8 cm). Cut the taped end into a gradual taper.

3. Lay the tapered end on the edge of the gourd. Anchor the primary color of yarn in one of the holes, then wrap it around the foundation material—the core—to secure it. Continue wrapping the core several times until you reach the second hole, then insert the needle, and continue wrapping until you reach the next hole.

4. When you want to change colors, move the primary yarn inside and select the next color. Wrap it around the core as you did in step 3 until you reach the next hole. Continue wrapping the core and anchoring it in the holes until you're ready for the next color.

5. Anchor each row to the one below it by inserting the needle through the yarn of the prior row after you complete each wrapping pattern.

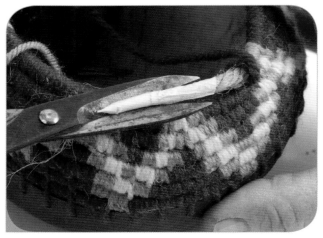

6. To end the coiling, gather the ends into a bundle and tape as you did in step 2, and cut into a gradual taper. Plan the taper so that it ends above the beginning taper.

7. Continue to coil until you reach the tape and tapered end of the core. Bury the end behind the last row, covering the end with wrapping yarn. By ending the row over the start of the weaving, the rim should remain horizontal.

GALLERY

Artist ● Gertrude Turner

Artist ● Robin Przybysz

Artist ● Gertrude Turner

Artist ● Stuart Fabe

ENDLESS WAVES

This variation on coiling is deceptively simple. It allows you to start your design lower on the gourd rather than right on the rim. You can create a range of stunning edges by using different materials.

WHAT YOU NEED

Small **GOURD**, cut, cleaned, and finished ● Small, motorized **CRAFT TOOL** with drill bits, or gourd or leather **AWL** ● Tapestry **NEEDLE** ● Waxed linen **THREAD** ● Leather **LACING** ● **FEATHERS**, beads, stones *(optional)*

WHAT YOU DO

1. Use the craft tool or awl to make holes around the gourd approximately 1 to 1½ inches (2.5 to 3.8 cm) from the rim and 1 inch (2.5 cm) apart. Insert the tapestry needle threaded with the waxed linen thread into a hole from the inside out.

2. Make a simple buttonhole stitch. Insert the needle in the next hole to the left, but don't pull the thread tight to the shell; instead leave a loop. Take the needle through the loop and pull tight, positioning the loop inside the gourd, not on the edge.

Artist ● Mary Gayle Van Ingen

3. Make sure the loop of each stitch stays on the inside of the gourd and does not rest on the edge.

4. When you finish stitching around the edge, bring the needle to the outside through the hole where you took the first stitch. Hold the leather lacing against the waxed linen stitches and, with the needle, go over the leather, behind the lacing stitch, and under and around the lacing. Pull taut.

5. Continue around the gourd, bringing the waxed linen thread under, around and over the leather, behind the lacing stitch, and under, around and over the leather, pulling taut each time. When you get to the starting point, bury the end under the second row.

6. Keep adding rows of leather lacing, pushing them snug against the preceding row, to form a slightly waved effect.

7. When you get to the rim, knot the end of the waxed linen inside the gourd around the stitches, and bury the end of the leather lacing under the coiling. You can also keep the lacing long for attaching embellishments, such as feathers, beads, or stones.

CHAPTER 5

TWINING

Twining is the traditional basket making technique of weaving various flexible materials, known as weavers or strands, around spokes. Creating the means for twining on gourds is all about adapting the shell: You can insert spokes into the shell and glue them in place, you can fashion spokes from the shell itself by cutting into the gourd to make slits for weaving, or you can remove parts of the shell to make wider pieces that resemble splints.

The weavers you use, much like the weft in weaving, pass around the spokes to create the pattern. You can use just about any flexible material for weavers, whether natural or man-made. Spokes that you insert into the shell can be rigid or soft, and you can use reeds, splints, twigs, rush, rope, or even wire.

Unlike traditional weaving, where you pass one weft element through the warp, twining can employ one, two, three, or more weavers that alternately go behind and in front of the spokes to encircle them. While the weavers usually completely cover the spokes, many artists add beads or leave spaces between the rows to expose the spokes or create irregular rows of weaving.

Twining Techniques on Gourds

If you're just learning how to twine, it's better to begin with a project that uses rigid spokes and one or two flexible weavers. As you increase your skills, you can experiment with different materials or add an additional weaver for three-strand twining.

PREPARING THE GOURD

To prepare a gourd for twining, you need to first secure the spokes. If the gourd's shell is thick enough, you can drill holes that are slightly smaller than the diameter of the spokes *into* the cut edge of the gourd. You insert the spokes into the holes and glue them in place. Once the glue has completely dried and set, you're ready to begin twining.

If you're working with a gourd with a thin shell, it's better to drill the holes *through* the shell. You dampen the spokes to make them flexible before inserting them into the holes with half the length on the inside and half on the outside of the gourd. To keep the spokes in an upright position, you can tape or tie them together. You can weave either against the shell of the gourd, or along its cut edge. You can also fasten the spokes to the sides of the gourd with a thin thread to utilize the uneven ends of the spokes as decorative elements.

TWINING BASICS

There are several factors that control twining patterns: whether you have an odd or even number of spokes, the color of the weavers, the number of weavers, and how you alternate the twist between spokes to determine which weaver is on the top or bottom after the crossover. The examples on pages 66 and 67 demonstrate simple twining with a few variations.

Slit Weaving

This technique allows incredible versatility. You make your own spokes or warp from the gourd itself by simply cutting slits into the shell. This provides you with built-in rigid structures around which you can twine or weave. You can use just about any material imaginable for the weavers or strands.

An important consideration to keep in mind before you cut the slits is whether you will have an odd or even number. If you plan on using a single weaver to make a plain weave, then you must cut an odd number of slits. If you're using two weavers, you can have either an even or odd number of slits.

It's fun to experiment. You can create patterns by using more than one color of weaver to make stripes, or you can change the weavers during the weaving process to create horizontal banding. You can also find weaving patterns in books or online that you can adapt to your liking. Once you feel comfortable with the technique, you can create an unlimited number of your own patterns and designs.

Splint Work

In its broadest definition, splint work refers to any basket made of wide splints used for both the spokes and weavers. For splint work on a gourd, you remove pieces of the shell to create wide spokes. You can then wrap or cover them with splints cut from more flexible material, using just about any weaving pattern you can adapt—from plain weaves to intricate twills.

The splints you use for the weavers can be made of many materials, including barks, strips of wood, leather, or folded paper. You can even use soft metal strips, which you loop, bend, or twist into shape, to create patterns that wouldn't otherwise be woven on a basket. Many artists create complex designs by varying the width and color of the weavers, or by folding or twisting the weavers to add textural interest.

Artist ● Ginger Summit

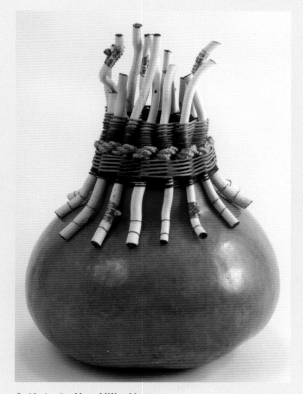

Artist ● Kay Hille-Hatten

Simple Weave

This technique is most effective when you have an odd number of spokes. A single weaver goes over one spoke, under the next, over the next, and so on.

Artist ● Kay Van Hoesen

Two-Strand Twining

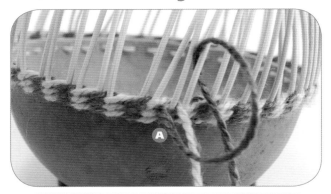

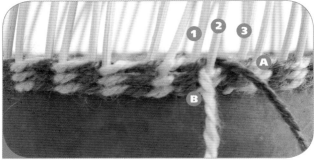

1. This color pattern produces vertical bands because the gourd has an even number of spokes. Weaver A goes in front of spoke 1 and behind spoke 2 while staying above weaver B.

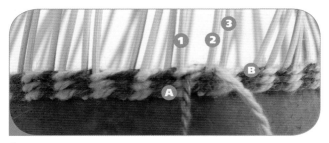

2. Weaver B goes in front of the first spoke and behind the second spoke while staying above weaver A.

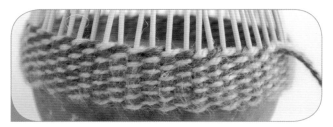

3. If you want a pattern with diagonal stripes, start with an odd number of spokes, and then work steps 1 and 2.

Three-Strand Twining

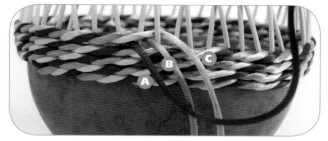

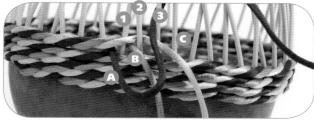

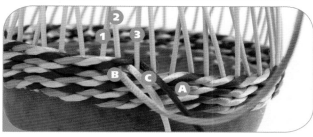

1. Weaver A passes above weavers B and C. Weaver A goes in front of spokes 1 *and* 2, and then behind spoke 3 while staying above weavers B and C. Weaver B is now in position for the next step.

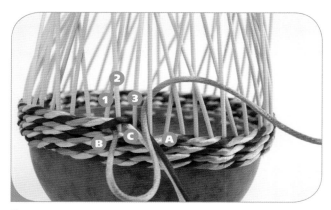

2. Weaver B goes in front of two spokes and behind the third spoke while staying above weavers C and A. Weaver C is now in position.

3. Weaver C goes in front of two spokes and behind the third while staying above weavers A and B. Note: You can add additional weavers. However, the spaces you skip by crossing the additional spokes may become unstable, depending on the materials you use.

FINISHING

Once you finish twining, you'll have spokes extending from the top of your completed course. Occasionally, artists choose to leave these ends free, painting them a complementary color, or embellishing them with beads, feathers, or fancy yarns as a cap to the twining itself. More often, they crimp the ends at the top of the twining, bend the ends over, and weave them back into the piece.

Once you complete the twined rim, attach pods and beads around the top edge to create a naturally frilled effect. You can add a medallion for even more flourish. If you wish to alter the design, try using two weavers made of cord instead of leaves.

WHAT YOU NEED

GOURD with a thick shell, cut, cleaned, and **FINISHED** ● **WATSONIA** leaves ● **#4 ROUND** reed ● Small, motorized **CRAFT TOOL** with drill bits ● White **GLUE** ● Needle-nose **PLIERS** ● Pods, beads, and **MEDALLION**

WHAT YOU DO

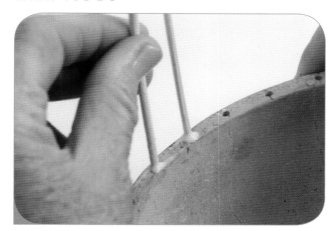

1. Soak the Watsonia leaves in water until flexible. Cut the #4 round reed into lengths, each 12 inches (30.5 cm) long. Use the drill to make holes in the edge of the gourd, spacing them approximately ½ inch (1.3 cm) apart. Fill each hole with white glue, and insert a piece of reed. Allow the glue to dry.

2. Place the ends of three Watsonia leaves in three adjacent spaces between the spokes. Note: If desired, you can work with two weavers for two-strand twining instead.

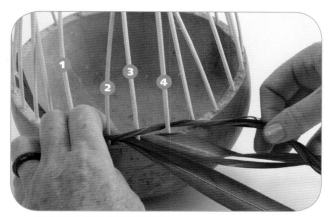

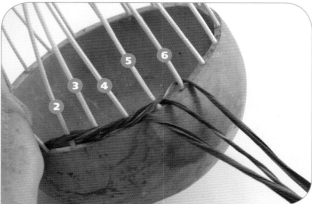

3. Twist the first Watsonia leaf, and bring it over the other two leaves and behind the fourth spoke. Twist the next leaf, and bring it over the other two leaves and around the fifth spoke. Do the same with the third leaf, twisting it and bringing it around the sixth spoke. Continue in this manner around the rim.

5. When you're finished twining, use the needle-nose pliers to crimp the spokes before bending them to place the ends inside. You may need to dampen the spokes first to make them more flexible. Twine the ends of the spokes around each other to finish. If you need to trim the spokes, allow them to dry thoroughly. If desired, dye the spokes to match the color of the leaves.

6. Finish the gourd by gluing the pods along the top edge. When dry, stitch beads to the pods as desired, and then glue on the medallion.

4. When you need to add another leaf, simply place the new leaf under the short end in the space between spokes, and twist the ends together. Cut the short end on the inside of the gourd, and continue twining with the new length.

Artist ● **Mary Simmons**

Artist ● **Marjorie Albright**

twining
weaving
plaiting

TRI-COLOR RUSH TRI-COLOR RUSH TRI-COLOR RUSH TRI-COLOR

TRI-COLOR RUSH TRI-COLOR RUSH TRI-COLOR RU

SH TRI-COLOR RUSH TRI-COLOR RUSH TRI-COLOR RUSH TRI

In many cultures, you frequently see gourds inside baskets that have been woven around them. The origin of this is unknown. Perhaps the basket protected a gourd from breakage or was merely an early device for attaching a handle. This project twines around soft spokes.

WHAT YOU NEED

GOURD ● 300 feet (90.9 m) of ⁵⁄₃₂" **FIBER RUSH** in golden brown ● **T-PINS** ● Masking **TAPE** ● 50 feet (15.2 m) each of ⁵⁄₃₂" **FIBER RUSH** in red, purple, and blue

WHAT YOU DO

1. Keep the gourd intact. Cut 12 spokes from the golden brown fiber rush. Stack them six over six to make a cross. Using the same color rush, work a plain weave around the spokes to make the base. Start with over two and under two. As the base grows, switch to over one, under one. Secure your work to the gourd with T-pins as needed. Weave until the base covers the bottom of the gourd.

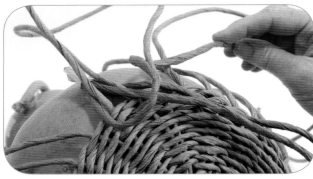

2. Gather one end of each of the colored rushes into a bundle, and wrap it with masking tape. Insert the loose strands, red first, purple next, then blue, from inside the weaving, with each color emerging from adjacent spaces between spokes. Bury the taped bundle between the weaving and the gourd.

3. Starting with the red strand, then the purple, then the blue, work three-strand twining. Pick up the red strand on the left, pass it in front of two spokes, behind the third, and bring it out between the next two adjacent spokes. It should exit in the space next to the blue weaving strand. Do the same for the purple strand, which should exit in the space next to the red strand. Finally do the same for the blue strand, which should exit next to the purple strand.

GALLERY

Artist ● **Kathy Rousso**

4. Continue the three-strand twining around the gourd three times. Keep the spokes against the gourd, and make sure the base of the weaving remains in contact with the bottom of the gourd. When you finish, move the ends of the three strands to the inside of the basket.

6. Cross each pair of spokes again and weave two more rows of two-strand twining with the colored strands. End the weaving with six rows of two-strand twining using the golden brown fiber rush. Keep the weaving tight against the gourd. Finish the gourd with a simple over two and in border.

Variation

5. Cross each pair of spokes and then weave two rows of two-strand twining.

You can see how easily you can attach a handle to the basket. The woven structure provides substantial support.

WOVEN ARROW WOVEN ARROW WOVEN ARROW WOVEN ARF
ROW WOVEN ARROW WOVEN ARROW WO
VEN ARROW WOVEN ARROW WOVEN ARROW WOVEN ARF

Once you cut the slits in the gourd, you automatically have your warp ready to go. Be sure you select a firm, hard gourd, since numerous cuts will weaken a lesser shell.

WHAT YOU NEED

GOURD, cut, cleaned, and finished ● **PENCIL** ● Small, motorized **CRAFT TOOL** with drill bits ● Small, motorized **JIGSAW** ● **SANDPAPER** ● Raffia **BRAID**, or weavers of choice

WHAT YOU DO

1. Use the pencil to mark upper and lower horizontal lines around the gourd to determine the length of the slits. Mark an odd number of vertical cutting lines for the slits, spacing them evenly around the gourd.

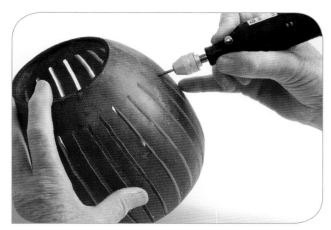

2. Drill a hole at the top and bottom of each line. Then either use the craft tool or motorized jigsaw to cut the line.

3. Use the sandpaper to sand in between the cuts to make sure they are even and smooth. If you round the edges of the interior shell as you sand, the weavers will lie nice and flat.

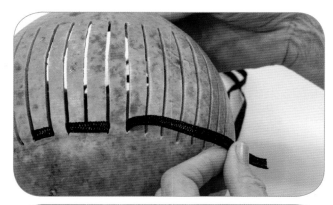

4. For this project, I used raffia braid to weave a reverse twill. First, bury the end on the inside of the gourd and secure it with tape. Begin the weaving with over one, under one, over two, and then begin the pattern of under one, over one, under one, and over two, and so on. Halfway up, reverse the pattern to create the arrow effect.

Artist ● **Don Weeke**

Artist ● **Jan Banta Briseno**
The artist wove a continuous length of seagrass cordage around the vessel.

BURNISHED BAMBOO

RNISHED BAMBOO BURNISHED BAMBOO BURNISHED BAMB
O BURNISHED BAMBOO BURNISHED E
SHED BAMBOO BURNISHED BAMBOO BURNISHED BAMBOO

This project borrows a technique from Asian basketry that inserts pieces of bamboo strips between spokes rather than weaving them. Heat from a torch eases the curve of the bamboo to the gourd—it also leaves random burn marks that add interest to the piece.

WHAT YOU NEED

GOURD, cut, cleaned, and finished ● Small, motorized **CRAFT TOOL** with drill bits, or gourd or leather **AWL** ●
Small, motorized **JIGSAW** ● **BAMBOO STRIPS** ● Propane **TORCH** with a flame spreader ● Small garden
CLIPPERS ● Insulated oven **GLOVE**

WHAT YOU DO

1. Prepare the gourd by marking the cutting lines around the shell. Use the motorized jigsaw to cut pieces from the shell, leaving wide splints.

2. You can give a permanent curve to the bamboo strips by steaming them or heating them with the propane torch, then letting them cool in or on a form. For this project, I clamped the bamboo to a cooking pot with the desired radius for the curve of the strips. After the strips cool, use the small garden clippers to cut them to size.

3. Insert the re-formed bamboo strips into the slots of the gourd. Carefully fit them in place, leaving one open slot between the insertions.

4. Insert a second strip to cross over the first. Then, moving to the right, insert the third strip in the open space to the right of the initial insertions. Insert the fourth strip to cross over both strips. Then insert the fifth strip just below the previous insertion. Continue this pattern around the gourd.

5. If the curve of the strips is not quite right, heat the strips with the propane torch equipped with a flame spreader.

6. While the strips are still hot, massage and push the strips into the correct shape. Make sure you wear the insulated oven glove to protect your hand. To complete the design, separate the top and bottom bands of diagonal pattern with two rows of horizontal insertions. **Note:** Our sources for the bamboo strips were salvaged from a bamboo placemat and an old bamboo shade.

Variation

This variation shows a different approach to the insertion technique. Notice the narrower slots cut in the gourd and the use of wider strips made of eucalyptus bark. You can insert the strips any way you want to create your own twill patterns. A band of plain weave in a darker color separates the twills, providing an opportunity to reverse the slant of the insertions for more interest.

Artist ● **Jim Widess**

Artist ● **Jill Walker**

TWINING

twining
weaving
plaiting

LONG DISTANCE LONG DISTANCE LONG DISTANCE LONG DIST
LONG DISTANCE **LONG DISTANCE** LONG DISTANCE LONG D
LONG DISTANCE LONG DISTANCE LONG DISTANCE LONG DIS

This wire technique
is the same the Zulus
use to make the
famous Zulu platters
and baskets. It's
employed here to
create a colorful and
sculptural closing for
a painted gourd bowl.

WHAT YOU NEED

GOURD, cut, cleaned, and painted ● Gourd or leather **AWL** ● 22-gauge **TELEPHONE WIRE** in multiple colors

WHAT YOU DO

1. Prepare the gourd by using the awl to punch an even number of holes in the shell, approximately ⅜ inch (9.5 mm) from the edge of the rim and ½ inch (1.3 cm) apart.

2. Cut five lengths each from the different colors of the telephone wire, each 48 inches (121.9 cm) long. Group the wires by colors. Insert one length of wire halfway through a hole in the gourd from the inside, then insert the other half of the wire through the adjacent hole so that both ends exit from the outside of the gourd and are of the same length. Organize the wires to prevent tangling.

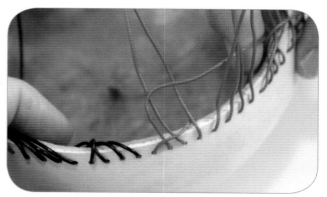

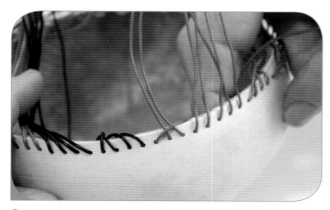

3. The weaving is fairly consistent as you work around the row. Pick up one wire and pass it in front of the two adjacent wires to the right and then behind the rest of the wires toward the inside of the shell.

4. Pick up the next wire to the right, pass it in front of the next two adjacent wires. Then pass the wire behind the rest of the wires to the right. Pick up the third wire to the right, pass it in front of the next two wires to the right and then behind the rest of the wires.

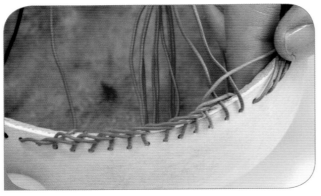

5. Continue this pattern all the way around the gourd rim. Treat the different colors as if they were all the same color as you weave.

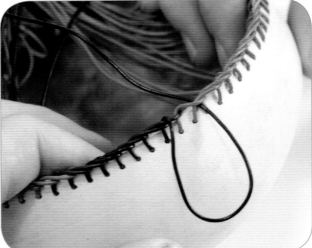

6. Once you've gone all the way around the rim, you're ready to close the gap between the first and last wires.

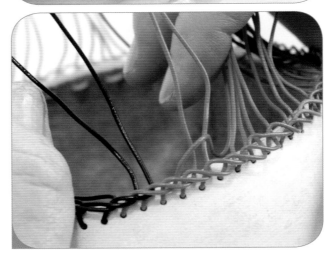

7. Pass the next to the last wire to the right in front of the last wire and the first wire. Then pass this wire to the inside. Pass the last wire in front of the first wire and the second wire, and then pass it to the inside. This completes the first row. Lift all of the wires so they are vertical once again, and repeat the weaving pattern for the next row.

8. To shape the top, tighten your weaving tension. If you want to reverse the color pattern, change the direction of the weave from moving to the right (counterclockwise) to moving to the left (clockwise).

9. To make the rim, change the weave to pass a wire behind two adjacent wires and then toward the outside of the shell instead of the inside. This small change locks the wires in place. When you've completed the rim, lift the wires to the vertical position.

WIRE WEAVING

Wire as a textile element was a rare and highly prized material for many hundreds of years in southern Africa. Because the process of making wire was laborious and complex, its use in ornament and embellishment gave value and esteem to common objects.

People valued copper and brass wires because of their golden color, but they also used nickel wire as well. With the building boom of the 1950s, laborers discovered telephone wire in abundance on job sites. They adapted their traditional weaving skills used for making baskets from native grasses to making baskets from this colorful, versatile wire.

Because wire is both flexible and able to hold a shape, combining the properties of strands and spokes, rigid spokes are unnecessary. Instead, you can twist the elements around each other to make the pattern rather than weaving around the spokes.

South Africa collection of Larry and Cordelia Raymond

Artist ● traditional
Zulu wire-covered gourd from the collection of Larry and Cordellia Raymond.

CHAPTER 6

WEAVING AND PLAITING

You can add rich textures or vibrant designs to a gourd with weaving and plaiting. Both techniques interweave strands of fiber that follow a variety of patterns and sequences. One feature distinguishing plaiting from weaving is that the warp and the weft are usually of equal width; in weaving, the warp and weft may or may not be of equal width.

Using these techniques can take many different forms. You can attach fiber warp elements to the shell to create the base for weaving a pattern or a tapestry. Or, you can borrow from basketry techniques to weave a random pattern around a gourd using reed, cane, or other plant fibers.

Weaving variations work well on gourds. Teneriffe uses a needle to pass the weft around a circular warp. And String Art, popularized in the 1960s, wraps string or yarn around fixed points multiple times to build a design. It takes on a whole new look when you work it over an opening cut into the shell.

One of the most recognizable forms of plaiting is simple braiding. But it can also encompass all kinds of plain and twill weaves. Covering a gourd with plaited leather strips creates a dramatic, sculptural piece.

Artist ● Ginger Summit

Artist ● Cindy Lee

Tapestry Weaving

The basic structure of tapestry weaving is plain weave, a simple under one, over one technique. Because the warp in tapestry is often thinner than the weft, the weft covers the warp. However, artists often expose a warp to enhance a design.

Tapestry weavers generally work from a cartoon, also called a cartouche, of the pattern, which they keep behind the upright warp. They use it as a map for following the changing colors of the design. When weaving a tapestry on a gourd, you can easily draw a cartoon of your design right on the shell using chalk or colored pencils.

When you're ready to weave, you can use one color and continue weaving in the same direction. Or, you can choose to create short rows of the same or different colors to build a design element. Where blocks of color meet, you can loop the ends around each other or you can leave a space between the sections. You can see this latter technique on Kilim rugs of the Middle East.

You thread the warp through holes you make in the shell. You can also stretch the warp across an opening or cutout in the gourd. Adding beads or other embellishments to either the warp or weft during the weaving process offers even more design potential.

Random Weave

An easy way to step into basketry is to cover a gourd with random weave. The technique combines the fundamental elements of basket making and weaving. Because you're weaving free-form and not following an intricate pattern, you can let yourself go as you get acquainted with the materials and how to work with them.

To create the forms, you use flexible yet sturdy weavers, such as vines or round reed. Twist ties or pieces of flexible wire help you hold together the ribs that create the foundation of the basket while you weave the basic structure that covers the gourd. When the framework is complete, you can weave other materials, such as yarns, wire, and finer native fibers, into it.

GALLERY

Artist ● **Judy Dominic**
A gourd that has been random woven.

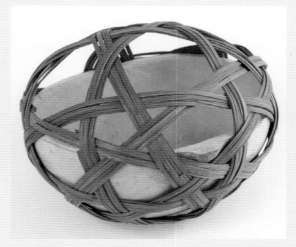

Artist ● **Stacey Speyer**
An example of plaited weave.

You can leave the weaving open, or entirely fill the spaces for a dense weave. Occasionally, artists use fancy yarns or other materials to twist around the crossovers, which add textural and decorative elements, as well as lending additional strength to the structure. You can also string beads on the weavers as you work, which the evolving woven structure will eventually hold in place.

Teneriffe

In traditional tapestry, the warp threads are vertical and parallel to each other. In Teneriffe, you stretch the warp threads across an open, usually round space, arranging them like the spokes of a wheel.

Teneriffe on a gourd most frequently spans a cutout in the side of the shell or lies across the top opening. Using a craft tool or awl, make small holes around the opening for stringing the warp. You can also stretch the warp across an uncut portion of the gourd to allow the weaving to lie on top of the shell.

You can weave using one color, or you can create colorful designs using many colors. You can completely cover the warp threads, or weave just portions leaving much of the warp exposed. By using thin or transparent cords for the warp, such as monofilament, you can make the design appear to be floating in space.

String Art

What can be easier than creating a work of geometric art by stretching thread or string over a grid of points? While mathematicians have struggled to create formulae to define the process, symmography is another name for string art. Crafters, from children to adults, continue to experiment with the variety of shapes and designs.

You can make many designs with this technique, but it's easiest to begin with a circle. Most often you would embed nails in a board or frame when making string art. When working on a gourd, it's easy to embed the nails directly into the shell. You can completely fill in the shape, or you can leave the center open. You can place any number of points on the circumference, but keep in mind that when the points are closer you'll have more threads and a denser design.

If you want to plan a design, draw a circle and place dots along its circumference. Then simply connect the dots with straight lines following a regular sequence around the circle. Once you've mastered the basic technique, experiment with different shapes and number of points to discover just how challenging this technique can be.

Plaiting

Interweaving elements equally, as you do in plaiting, presents a challenge. Since all the ends are essentially weavers with no one warp element, such as spokes, it can be frustrating to try to control the emerging shape while keeping the order of strands in mind. Clips, clamps, tape, and weights can help you hold portions of the work secure as you focus on the pattern sequence.

You can start many types of plaiting off the gourd. As the interlacing progresses, you slip it over either the top or the base of the gourd and gradually cinch it tight to envelop the shape of the vessel. You can work the ends into a base or rim, or you can work them back into the pattern to hide them in the weave.

One technique for beginning simple plaiting on a gourd is to anchor the strands in holes drilled into either the gourd's base or neck. Another is to first secure the strands on a separate thread, cord, or wire to anchor them, work the plaiting, and then secure the ends on a second similar anchor.

You can create many different patterns with plaiting by altering the weave structure of the strands, although they are usually based on a diagonal line. You can use different fibers when plaiting on gourds, but keep in mind that you want the elements to be somewhat flexible so the final result will fit snug to the gourd's surface.

Artist ● **Ellen Hendricks**

Artist ● **Ginger Summit**
Plaited rawhide around a gourd

Artist ● **Jill Walker**

The Inca cross is an important symbol in the Andes regions of Peru and Bolivia. You can find this image in many ruins and ancient artifacts. This geometric pattern lends itself beautifully to tapestry weaving.

WHAT YOU NEED

GOURD, cut, cleaned, and finished ● **PENCIL** ● Small, motorized **CRAFT TOOL** with drill bits, or gourd or leather **AWL** ● Colored **CHALK** or **PENCILS** ● Waxed linen **THREAD** ● Tapestry **NEEDLE** ● **YARN** in assorted colors ● **BUTTON** *(optional)*

WHAT YOU DO

1. Use the pencil to draw two lines around the gourd that are the width of the desired tapestry. Mark points along the lines that are opposite each other and evenly spaced. Use the craft tool or awl to make holes in the shell at these points.

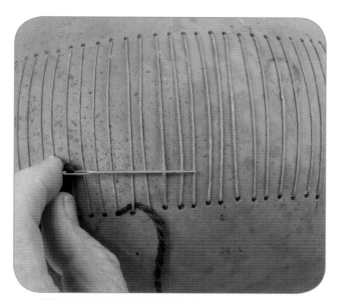

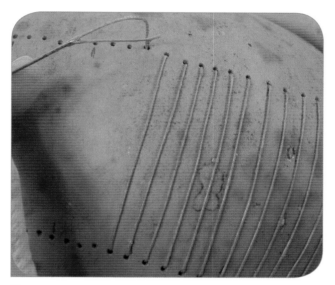

2. Draw a cartoon of your design on the shell using the colored chalk or pencils. Using the tapestry needle and waxed linen thread, stitch though the holes to stretch the warp. Make sure to pull the thread taut.

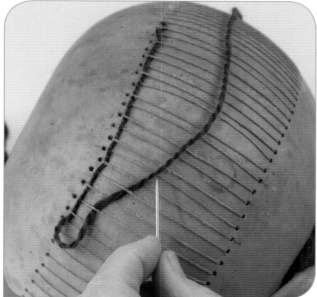

3. Bury the end of the first color inside the gourd. Then begin weaving over and under the warp threads. In this example, I started with the blue interior of the design and then added the black.

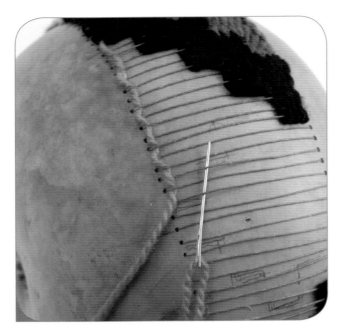

4. To add a new color, bury the end of the new thread under the weaving already created, and continue weaving.

5. Where the colors meet, you can either wrap the second colored yarn around the same warp thread, or pull it through the loop of the first color. Continue building the pattern by weaving back and forth over each area until you've covered the entire warp.

6. To complete the rim, drill or punch holes in the shell approximately 1 inch (2.5 cm) from the edge. Thread the tapestry needle with black thread or yarn, and sew through the holes to wrap the rim.

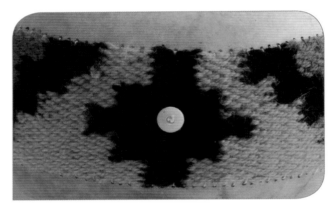

7. Traditionally, the center of an Inca Cross is a hole. However, I sewed a button on it to complete the design.

tip ⟶ You can cover as much or as little of the gourd with tapestry as you wish. It's completely up to you, and can depend on the shape of the gourd and the design you're using.

Artist ● Gertrude Turner

Artist ● Marjorie Albright

Artist ● Marla Helton

Artist ● Kathy Riker

weaving
plaiting

AT RANDOM AT RANDOM AT RANDOM AT RANDOM AT RANDOM AT RAN
AT RANDOM AT RANDOM AT RANDOM AT RANDOM AT RANDOM AT RAN
AT RANDOM AT RANDOM AT RANDOM AT RANDOM AT RANDOM AT RAN

This round gourd is covered in a dense weave. If desired, you can weave a more open pattern by using fewer foundation ribs and weavers. Beads can enhance the beauty of the random design.

WHAT YOU NEED

Small round **GOURD** ● Natural **VINES**, such as willow or wisteria ● Twist **TIES** or flexible **WIRE** ● **BEADS** or other embellishments *(optional)*

WHAT YOU DO

1. Begin wrapping the foundation ribs around the gourd. Use the twist ties or short lengths of the flexible wire to secure the basic framework. Note: You may need to presoak the vines for extra flexibility. This project uses wisteria vines.

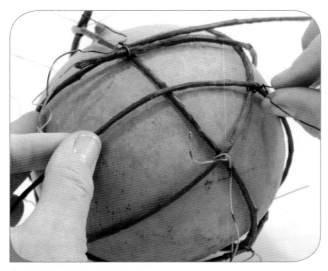

2. Use twist ties to secure all the beginning crossovers. Continue to create several ribs by changing the path of vines until they roughly define the shape of the piece. Use twist ties to hold the ribs in place wherever they cross.

3. Once you've created the foundation, begin weaving with another piece of vine. Weave over and under the ribs, as well as the weaver strand. Move the weaver in one direction, in a circular pattern, or in random directions for different effects.

4. Gradually remove the twist ties or wire as you secure the ribs in place with the weavers. Continue interlacing with weaver strands until you achieve your desired effect. You can string beads on the weavers as you work for added embellishment.

Basket Variation

Artist ● **Ginger Summit**

If you want to make a basket, start with a cut, cleaned, and finished gourd. For the rim, cut a length of vine to the diameter of the gourd's opening. Make a random woven "wreath" the same diameter as the gourd opening. Begin with a circle of vine the appropriate diameter, and then wrap this three or four times with the end of the vine (or other material if desired). The wraps can go under and over each other in random sequence so it doesn't look like a plain wrapped ring. Wrap the vine with one or more of the materials you will use for the random weave. Begin your random weave on the gourd, incorporating the rim as you work. Work any loose ends from the rim's wrapping into the random weave.

Make the handle by wrapping a length of vine as you did for the rim. Leave a generous length of the wrapping materials extending from each end of the vine. Use the ends to attach the handle to the rim. When you've secured the handle, cut off any extra length of the wrapping or weave the ends into the random weave on the gourd.

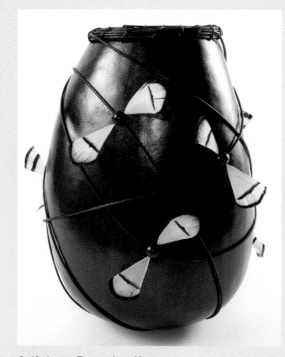

Artist ● **Browning House**

weaving
plaiting

BRIGHT SPIRAL BRIGHT SPIRAL BRIGHT SPIRAL BRIGHT SPIRA
RAL BRIGHT SPIRAL **BRIGHT SPIRAL** BRIGHT SPIRAL BRIG
T SPIRAL BRIGHT SPIRAL BRIGHT SPIRAL BRIGHT SPIRAL B

Creating richly colored Teneriffe patterns on a gourd is as simple as making holes in the shell and stringing radial spokes. The art is in the selection of the spokes through which to pass the needle and thread. The number of possible designs—infinite.

> Designer ● Marjorie Albright

WHAT YOU NEED

GOURD, cut, cleaned, and finished ● Small, motorized **JIGSAW** ● Small, motorized **CRAFT TOOL** with drill bits, or gourd or leather **AWL** ● Waxed linen **THREAD** ● Tapestry **NEEDLE** ● **YARN**

WHAT YOU DO

1. Use the motorized jigsaw to cut a circle from the side of the gourd. Use the craft tool or awl to make holes around the circle approximately ¼ to ⅜ inch (6 mm to 9.5 mm) in from its edge. You can make either an even or odd number of holes.

2. Anchor one end of waxed linen thread in one hole. Thread the other end on the tapestry needle. Bring the thread across the circle to the hole directly opposite, pass the thread through it, and pull it taut. Bring this warp thread back to the hole on the right, next to the starting point. Continue around the circle, completely filling it with threads that cross at the center point— think spider web.

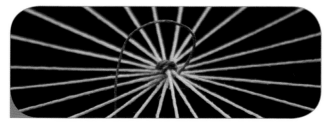

3. If you have an even number of holes, you can tie off the warp in the last hole and begin weaving with a new strand. If you have an odd number of holes, your last warp strand will end at the center, which works well if you're using the same thread for weaving. With either a new strand or the end of the warp, wrap around the meeting point of the spokes a few times to tighten the center.

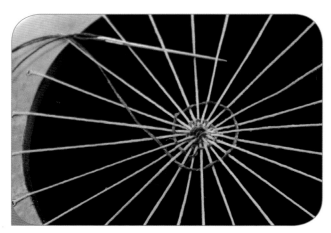

4. Begin the plain weave—over one, under one, and so on—around the center. Note: For the first several rows, you may need to weave over and under multiple warp threads because they are so close together at the center point. As you work farther from the center, begin weaving over and under one. Depending on the effect you want, you can pull the strand tight to the center or weave it more loosely.

5. I made a dense circle at the center by tightly pulling the strand as I wove four or five passes around the center. Once you've woven the center, you can build out your design with weaving. Start working the plain weave over four warp threads for several rows.

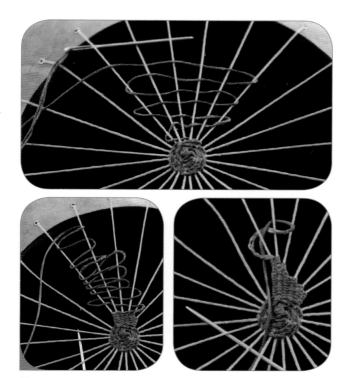

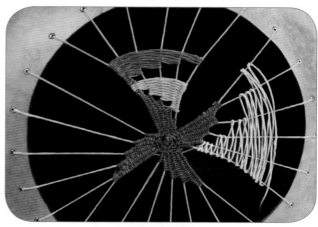

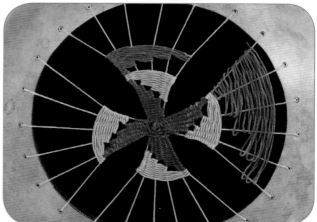

6. Shape the design by adding and subtracting the number of warp threads you weave over. You can expand the weave by adding two more warp threads to the weaving. Likewise, you can reduce the weave by subtracting two warp threads. You can see the evolving pattern in the tightened weave.

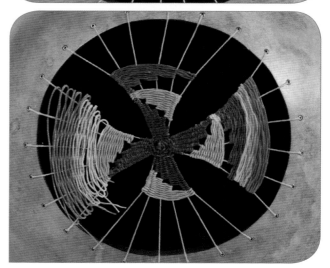

7. When starting a new color or a new section of pattern, bury the end of the weaver in the existing weaving.

8. Continue weaving in sections, changing colors as desired, to complete your design.

THE ART OF TENERIFFE

Gourd artist Betty Blakley has taken Teneriffe in new directions. Her use of color in addition to her unique designs creates exciting ways for thinking about this technique. Notice that Betty doesn't always space her holes exactly the same distance apart. She's worked out many patterns, and often drills the holes to give form to the designs.

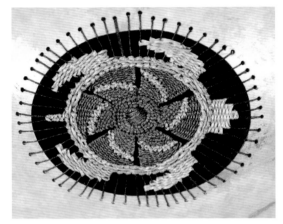

Artist ● Ellen Hendricks

Artist ● Mary Simmons

String art on gourds
provides depth to an
intriguing geometric
pattern. For even
more fun, try stringing
wire or some of the
newer man-made
fibers for a totally
different look.

WHAT YOU NEED

GOURD with a thick shell, cut, cleaned, and finished ● Small **NAILS** or **BRADS** ● Waxed linen **THREAD** in various colors

WHAT YOU DO

1. Mark the placement for the nails or brads on the circumference of the cut edge. If you want to completely close the center of the shape, mark an even number. If you want a slight opening in the center, mark an odd number. Firmly embed the nails or brads in the edge, and tie one end of the waxed linen thread to one of them.

2. I worked this design with a space in the center to show the fossils I glued inside. Bring the thread only partially around the circumference of the gourd, not to the point directly opposite. Count the nails between the anchored end and the first loop around the nail, and count the same number of nails to the third loop.

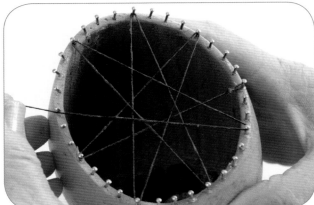

3. Continue in this manner around the opening until you've circled all the nails. Notice the hole in the center created by the stringing pattern.

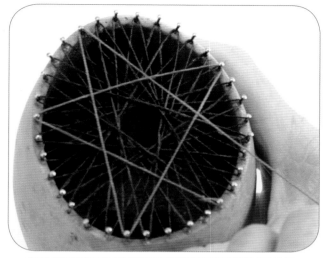

4. Tie the first string for the second layer to a nail. Bring the string only partially around the opening, and loop it around a nail at that point. Count the number of nails between these two points, and then count the same number from the second nail. Loop around this nail, and follow the sequence until you've wrapped all of the nails.

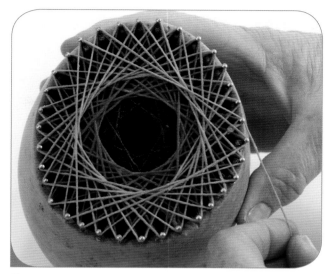

5. You can continue to add multiple layers. If each layer has a smaller number of nails between wrapping points, you'll create a larger opening in the center to reveal the previous layers.

6. Once you've completed all layers, twine a strand around the nails to frame the design.

tip ⟶ If you want to completely fill in the center of the first layer, take the first string across the opening to the nail directly opposite and firmly loop it around. Next take the string to the closest nail on the right side of the beginning nail, and loop the string firmly around. Continue in this manner until you've filled the entire circle.

Artist ● **Lynette Dawson**

Artist ● **Lynette Dawson**

Artist ● **Lynette Dawson**

weaving
plaiting

I DREAM OF GENIE I DREAM OF GENIE I DREAM OF GENIE I DI
GENIE **I DREAM OF GENIE** I DREAM OF GENIE I DREAM OF
NIE I DREAM OF GENIE I DREAM OF GENIE I DREAM OF GEI

Most of us remember
braiding from childhood.
It's a form of plaiting
and can range from very
simple to complex,
depending on the braiding
pattern and the number
of strands you use.

WHAT YOU NEED

Bottle **GOURD**, cut, cleaned, and finished ● **LEATHER** strips in two different colors ● Waxed linen **THREAD** or **WIRE** ● **TAPE** ● Rubber **BANDS** ● Wood or metal **RING** for the base

WHAT YOU DO

1. Cut an equal number of lengths from each color of the leather strips. Make each length approximately three to three-and-one-half times the length of the gourd you're covering.

2. Secure the waxed linen thread or wire around the neck of the gourd as an anchor for the strips. Slip the end of a strip under the thread or wire, and pull until one half is hanging from either side of the anchor. Repeat this step, alternating the colors of the strips around the anchor.

3. Select two adjoining strips of different colors, and cross them. In plaiting, the weaving, or braiding, is done on the diagonal, with one of each of the pairs of cords going to the left and the other end going toward the right.

4. With the next neighboring strip, go under and over the crossed ends. Continue in this manner, taking the end of the next strip and weaving it over and under the previously woven strips.

5. If you find you need to add additional strips, secure in place with a rubber band the work you've already completed, and add strips under the anchor. The number of strips you use will depend on the density of plaiting desired.

6. Continue to work your way around, cinching the strands tight as you go. Rotate the gourd as you work to keep the plaiting at approximately the same level around the gourd. You may need to hold the already-woven ends in place using tape or rubber bands. As the diameter changes, loosen the plaiting to accommodate the widening area while keeping the pattern even.

7. Wrapping the ends around a ring at the bottom of the gourd creates a solid base and provides an easy way to tie off the ends.

8. I used the Turks head knot to cover a ring for the neck, which I slipped over the gourd and cinched in place. You can also wrap the neck with a strip of leather to hide the anchor cord, and add beads to complete the project.

tip ➜ You don't need to limit yourself to plaiting with leather. Try other materials, including various types of cording and ribbon. Using three or more colors also produces some interesting results.

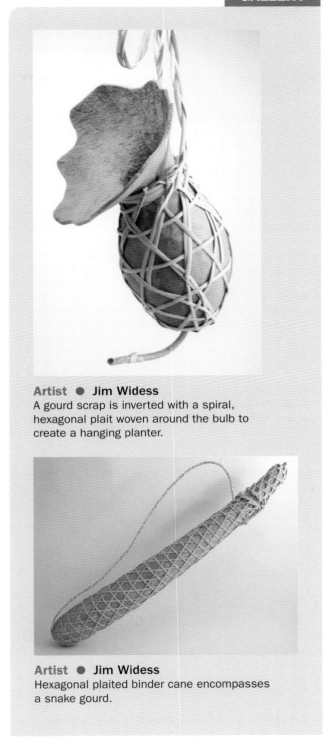

Artist ● Jim Widess
A gourd scrap is inverted with a spiral, hexagonal plait woven around the bulb to create a hanging planter.

Artist ● Jim Widess
Hexagonal plaited binder cane encompasses a snake gourd.

PLATING

CHAPTER 7

NETTING AND KNOTTING

One of the first uses of fiber on gourds was probably some form of netting that helped people better grasp or carry the vessel. Cultures developed their own variations on this basic technique that works one element in a series of continuous loops to make a mesh structure. Some netting techniques include knotting, while others are simply a series of interlocking loops that gives them the name knotless netting.

Knotting is a close cousin to looping and came later in the evolution of techniques. Knotting on a gourd creates a surrounding mesh much like looping, but it employs two or more elements that interlace to create the knots that define the structure. Macramé popularized knot craft, and many of the simplest knots, such as the half hitch, lark's head, and the square knot are basic to knotting on gourds.

While the original uses of netting and knotting were primarily functional, artists today have expanded the techniques to include many decorative applications, from covering the entire exterior of a gourd to filling in openings or holes cut into the shell. Likewise, artists use a wide variety of traditional and new materials, including leather, natural fibers, yarns, and wire.

Knotless Netting

This ancient textile technique creates a sturdy interlaced mesh without the use of knots. Artisans often refer to it as looping or needlelace. It's possible that early cultures made net bags to slip over gourds for ease of carrying. But it soon became apparent that working the netting directly on the gourd itself made the net more secure and could protect the shell as well as provide a handle.

You can start the netting on the gourd by anchoring the strands in holes you make in the rim. Or, you can secure a taut cord or wire to the gourd that acts as a base cord for anchoring the strands.

Because knotless netting is so flexible, you can add and subtract loops to shape the pattern, as well as pull them taut to make the netting fit snug against the gourd. The netting can be open or dense, and you can add textured effects by the way you loop. Adding beads or shells to the netting also creates added interest.

Knotted Netting

You can see this eons-old technique in both historic and contemporary examples. Unlike knotless netting, which uses one working strand, knotted netting employs many vertical strands that you knot together to create the structure. Before you begin knotting, you secure a base cord around the top of the gourd, and then anchor the working strands to it.

Knots range from simple overhand knots to fancy knotwork often identified with Oriental textiles and crafts. Another variation, which people may not identify with knotted netting, is the familiar craft of macramé. If you're not familiar with how to make some of the basic knots, see Know Your Knots on page 122.

Macramé

For those who remember macramé from the 1960s, it might conjure up memories of plant hangers, wall hangings, purses, and belts, all constructed primarily of variations on two knots—the double half hitch and the square knot. Today, you most often see macramé in gourd craft as a way to suspend containers for planters or birdhouses. However, there are many other ways to use the knots, along with basket-making techniques, to create artistic coverings for your gourd.

You start the macramé by attaching a base cord or ring to either the top or bottom of the gourd. Then a simple lark's head knot (page 122) secures the working strands to it. You knot the strands to partially or fully cover the gourd. When you leave spaces between your knots you create an openwork effect.

The versatile square knot (page 123) is popular in macramé. Because you work it using four strands—two alternately as anchor strands and two as working strands—you need to make sure the number of working strands is always a multiple of four. If you're incorporating the ends of the base cord into the design, make sure you add them to the count of working strands.

You can use any cord for knotwork, as long as you can pull it tight without it breaking. Some slippery cords, such as silk, may be more difficult to use if you're a beginner. Artists often create fascinating patterns combining different textures and types of cords, so you may want to consider using a variety of cords in the same project.

Beads and macramé seem to go together naturally. You can slip them on the working strands and knot around them, or you can secure them to the base cord as embellishment.

Fancy Knotwork

Closely related to macramé is another style of working with cords to create ornamental patterns. Technically they aren't knots, though that is what people commonly call them. They don't support weight or heavy tension, and you can't cinch the cords without distorting the decorative elements. The individual knots are known by many names, and because they're basic to Chinese, Celtic, and nautical traditions, it's difficult to trace their origins.

The simplest knot of this type, and the one that is the basis for many of these decorative pieces, is the Josephine knot (page 123), also known as the Carrick bend and double coin. It consists of two ends with intertwining loops. They don't actually form a knot, but you can pull the cords quite firmly to make a belt or decorative hanging.

Another ornamental knot of this type is one you frequently see on Japanese bamboo baskets and rattan teapot handles. You wrap and tuck a rattan strand around an element or object to create simple yet elegant ornamentation. The technique pairs beautifully with a green-scraped banana gourd.

GALLERY

Artist ● **contemporary**
Copper wire is netted around a gourd.

Artist ● **contemporary**
An egg gourd is netted with copper wire.

Artist ● **contemporary**
Netted silver wire extends the sides of this gourd.

netting
knotting

SHIMMERING NET SHIMMERING NET SHIMMERING NET SHIM
NG NET **SHIMMERING NET** SHIMMERING NET SHIMMERING
MERING NET SHIMMERING NET SHIMMERING NET SHIMM

The copper netting fairly glows against the dark-stained shell. By varying the space between the loops, you create this simple diamond shape—or have fun trying even fancier patterns.

WHAT YOU NEED

Small **GOURD**, cut, cleaned, and finished ● Gourd or leather **AWL** ● Tapestry **NEEDLE** ● Flexible copper **WIRE**

WHAT YOU DO

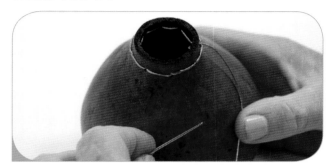

1. Use the awl to make holes around the opening of the gourd, spacing them approximately ½ inch (1.3 cm) apart. Thread the tapestry needle with the copper wire, and secure the end of the wire on the inside of the gourd at one hole. Stitch twice around the rim to fill all the spaces between holes. This is the anchor row.

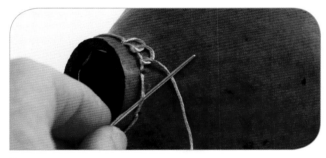

2. To begin the netting, bring the needle up and under the anchor row, gently pulling to create a small loop. Continue around the circumference of the gourd to make the first row of loops.

3. For the second row, put the needle into the first loop, and then gently pull to create a loop approximately the size of the loops in the first row. Continue in this manner to cover the gourd. If you run out of wire, twist the end of the new wire around the old, and bury the join in the netting.

4. As the diameter of the gourd increases, don't add additional loops; rather, allow the spaces between to expand. Once you pass the widest part of the gourd, begin cinching the loops to hug the shape of the gourd. When you get to the end, reduce the number of loops to entirely cover the bottom of the gourd.

5. Bury the end of the wire under the dense loops on the bottom. If desired, wrap a ring with copper wire to give the gourd stability as well as to provide an attractive base.

This technique creates a denser net than the previous project, Shimmering Net. By using a netting gauge, which you can purchase or cut from stiff cardboard, you keep the loops uniform in size.

WHAT YOU NEED

GOURD, cut, cleaned, and finished ● **PENCIL** ● Gourd or leather **AWL** ● 100 yards (90 m) of waxed **IMITATION SINEW** ● Tapestry **NEEDLE** ● Netting **GAUGES** ● **BEADS** or other embellishments

WHAT YOU DO

1. Use the pencil to mark evenly spaced holes around the neck of the gourd approximately ½ inch (1.3 cm) apart and ½ to ¾ inch (1.3 to 1.9 cm) from the rim, and then use the awl to make the holes. Thread the needle with the sinew, and stitch an anchor row by stitching twice around the rim to fill all the spaces.

2. For the first stitch, place the needle up under the second anchor stitch and back down under the first stitch to make a loop. You'll see the working strand is on top of the loop. Continue in this way to complete the first row. Don't pull the loops tight, and try to keep them uniform.

3. For the second row, put the needle behind the loops in the first row where the threads cross.

4. Don't pull the sinew tight, but allow the loops to increase in size as the diameter of the gourd increases. When you run out of sinew, add a new length by using a small knot to join the new to the old. Bury the knot under the rows of crossed threads.

5. Use netting gauges of appropriate widths to keep the loops loose and uniform in size. Slip the gauge inside each loop and then simply tighten the sinew around it.

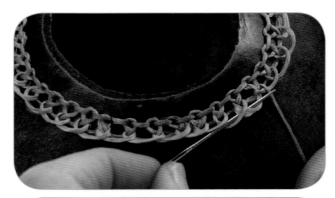

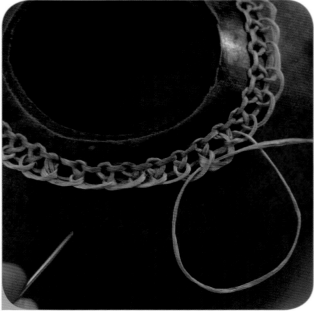

6. Continue adding rows, always placing the needle under the loops in the previous row where the threads have crossed. As you continue to cover the gourd, the netting will cinch firmly against the shell, and the pattern will emerge.

7. This is the bottom of the gourd. To finish the netting, continue to cinch the loops tighter and tighter at the bottom of the gourd until the rows of loops come together. Bind off by tying a knot in the last row, and then bury the end of the sinew under the netting.

8. String beads or attach other embellishments of choice between the anchor row and the first row of netting.

tip ——▶ You can purchase a set of netting gauges made of plastic, bone, or wood. But it's just as easy to make your own by cutting them from stiff cardboard.

LOOPING VARIATIONS

Artist Candy Krueger loves to experiment with variations on basic looping stitches. A curving long neck on a dipper gourd is the perfect canvas for her art. The images are details of a few of the individual stitches she worked around the necks of the gourds.

Artist ● **Candy Krueger**

Artist ● **Lois Rainwater**

Artist ● **Donna Kallner**

Artist ● **Sharon Wheat**

RIPPLED RIM

RIPPLED RIM RIPPLED RIM RIPPLED RIM RIPPLED RIM RIP
RIM RIPPLED RIM RIPPLED RIM RIPPLED RIM RIPPLED RIM RII
RIPPLED RIM RIPPLED RIM RIPPLED RIM RIPPLED RIM RII

You can use netting selectively to embellish a rim. The closer you position the holes, the more rippling the effect. This project uses a looping stitch that ends with a small knot at its base.

> Designer ● Marjorie Albright

WHAT YOU NEED

GOURD, cut, cleaned, and finished ● Gourd or leather **AWL** ● 2 tapestry **NEEDLES** ● 4-ply waxed linen **THREAD** in black, salmon, and dark rust

WHAT YOU DO

1. Use the awl to make holes approximately ½ inch (1.3 cm) from the edge. The closer you space the holes, the more rippling the edge. You can have an odd or even number of holes. The project on the left has an odd number, which creates diagonal twining; the project on the right has an even number, which creates vertical twining with a striped effect.

2. Thread one of the tapestry needles with a long length of the black waxed linen thread. Insert the needle from the inside of the gourd to the outside, leaving a 3-inch (7.6 cm) tail on the inside. Bring the thread over the edge and through the next hole. Make sure the needle passes through the loop of the previous stitch and over the working thread.

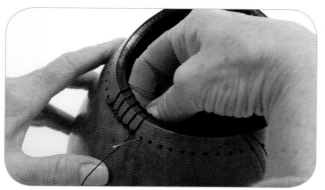

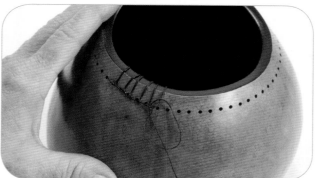

3. Snug the vertical thread, and place the knot so that it covers the hole. Then pass the working thread over the edge, and bring it from the inside out through the next hole. You can see the stitch that makes the knot in detail, and then several completed stitches.

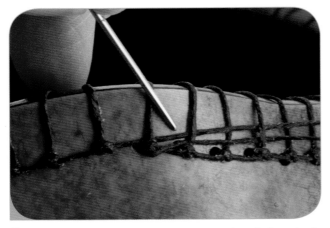

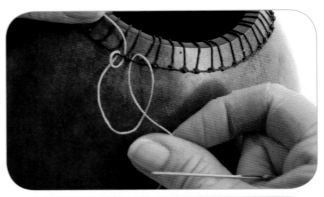

4. When you've gone all the way around, pull the 3-inch (7.6 cm) tail from the inside to the outside through the hole, and tie it off. Slip the tail under several vertical stitches; you'll hide the tail in the twining later on.

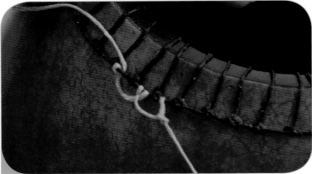

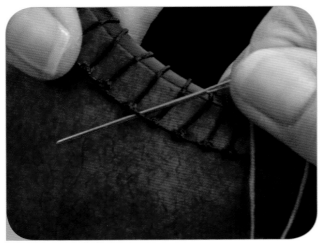

5. Thread a tapestry needle with the salmon thread. Work the rows using the same stitch you've been using; they'll look different because they don't span the edge. Pass the needle under the black thread. Loop the tail around to secure it, and then pass the working thread over the black thread and through the loop with the working thread on top.

6. Make even loops between each pair of vertical stitches. Continue knotting each loop—a loose half hitch (page 122)—as shown in the detail of the stitch in step 3, in between the knots of the previous row. Keep the loops just large enough for the rows to lie flat against the gourd. When you've completed two rows, tie off the end.

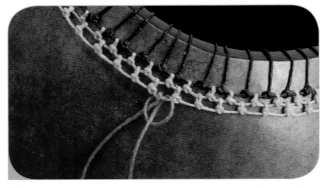

7. Thread the needle with the dark rust thread. To make the ripple effect, you'll stitch three loops into each of the loops from the previous row but *without* the knots.

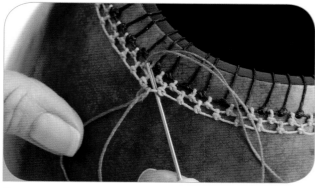

8. Make a simple loop through the loop of the previous row, and then make two more loops through the same loop. Repeat, making three loops in each of the following loops in the previous row.

9. Here you can see three stitches in each loop.

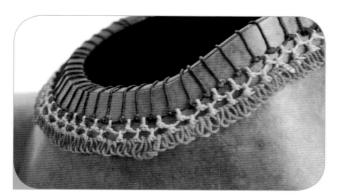

10. When you get back to the starting point, tie the two ends together to close the row and finish the ripple. Here you can see the completed row.

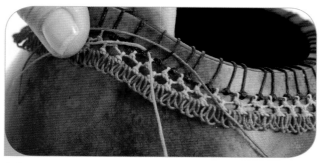

11. To begin the twining, thread a length of salmon thread on a needle and pass it under one of the vertical stitches, leaving a 6-inch (15.2 cm) tail to the left of the vertical stitch. Do the same with the dark rust thread on a separate needle, passing it under the next vertical stitch to the right, and leaving a tail.

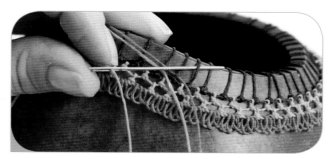

12. Begin twining with the salmon thread, passing it under the next stitch to the right of the dark rust thread. Pull the thread all the way through, and then let it hang. Pick up the needle with the rust thread, and go over the salmon thread and under the next stitch.

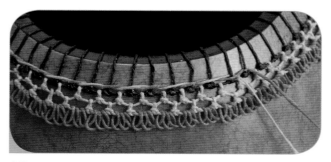

13. Continue alternating threads all the way around for several rows until you fill up the space between the knots and the edge of the rim.

tip ⟶ Continuous stitching can abrade the waxy layer on waxed thread, making it look a bit ragged. You can refresh and smooth the wax by passing a hair dryer over the threads. Don't get too close, and use a sweeping side-to-side motion for best results.

Scholars think the Incas embedded information into knotted strands, known as *khipu*, by the length and placement of the knots. For this project, you need only concern yourself with creating a decorative pattern from this simple technique.

WHAT YOU NEED

One tall bottle **GOURD**, cleaned and finished ● 20 yards (18 m) of cotton **CORD** ● Fabric **DYE** (optional)

WHAT YOU DO

1. Cut the cotton cord into lengths, each approximately three times the length of the gourd. Because you fold each length in half to make two working strands, you only need to cut as many cords as will loosely fit around half the gourd. If desired, use the fabric dye to dye the cords in a color or colors of your choice.

2. Cut and attach an anchor cord around the opening of the gourd. Then fold a cord in half and attach to the anchor cord using a lark's head knot (page 122). Attach all cords to the anchor in this way. For this project, I chose to make a wide knotted band of half-hitch knots (page 122) before beginning the khipu.

3. The basic knot used for khipu is an elongated overhand knot. Instead of just bringing the end through the loop a single time, bring it through multiple times. The more times you bring the end through, the longer the knot will become. Pull the knot gently, making sure the loops cinch together in a line.

SECRETS OF KHIPU

While the Incas never developed a true writing system, they did invent khipu, a system of communication using knotted strings. Khipu consisted of many strings that were fastened on an anchor thread, with knots placed in various spots along the lengths of the individual strings. Often sets of the strings were dyed different colors, which experts believe carried additional meanings. To this day, archaeologists and anthropologists still struggle to decode the Incas' highly effective yet elusive system. The specific meanings embedded in the knots have only recently been partially decoded. It is thought that khipu was used for accounting: keeping detailed records of population, tribute owed and paid, and tasks assigned.

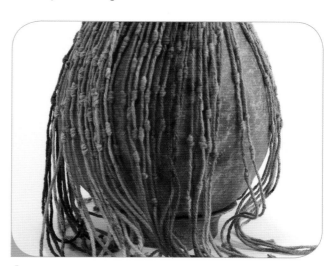

4. Continue in this way, creating knots of varying lengths along the cotton cords at varying heights.

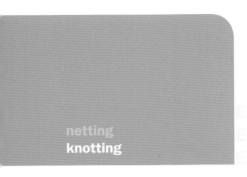

SHELL SHEKERE

This project uses small shells for the noisemakers. Even though they may be too delicate to hold up under much playing, they help create a simply beautiful showpiece.

WHAT YOU NEED

Intact dipper **GOURD** or bottle gourd, cleaned and finished ● **LEATHER** lacing, or rubber or metal **RING** ● 100 feet (30.3 m) of ¹⁄₁₆ inch (1.6 mm) drum **CORD**, waxed linen **THREAD**, or seine **TWINE** ● Gourd or leather **AWL** ● Small **SHELLS**, approximately 100 to 200 depending on the density of the knotting

WHAT YOU DO

1. Either make a ring to go around the neck of the gourd using the leather lacing, or use a purchased metal or rubber ring.

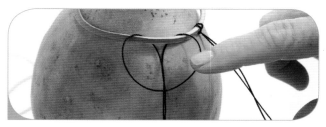

2. Cut the cord, thread, or twine at least four times the length of the project, measured from the ring to the end of the gourd. Each length will become two working strands. Cut enough lengths to fit *loosely* around the ring; you need to allow enough distance between the cords to accommodate the noisemakers.

3. Attach the cords to the ring using a lark's head knot (page 122), cinching the knots tight to the ring.

4. To secure the strands, tie an overhand knot with a pair of strands.

5. Use the awl to position the knot close to the ring before cinching it tight, then repeat around the ring.

SHEKERE!

This popular percussion instrument originated in sub-Saharan Africa. As musical traditions migrated with the slave trade, the instrument came to the Western Hemisphere. Today, music groups around the world use the shekere to shake out rhythms that get people dancing.

While you can use many different shapes and sizes of gourds to make a shekere, all have one thing in common—you knot the netting that covers the exterior, and you work the noisemakers into the netting as you knot. The materials you use to create the netting should be flexible enough to allow for free movement of the net against the gourd, but durable enough to endure vigorous shaking.

GALLERY

Artist ● Daniel Randolph Talibe

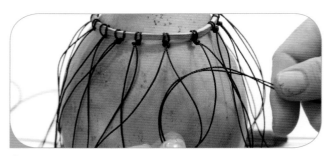

6. For the first row of knotting, tie one end from each pair of strands together using an overhand knot.

7. Again, use an awl if necessary to ensure that you evenly space the knots around the gourd.

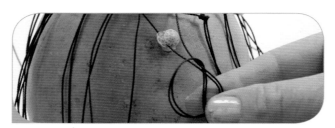

8. Begin adding the shells on the second row. String a shell on one strand of the pair, and then make your overhand knot. The stringing design is up to you. If the shells are small, try stringing one on each strand before tying the knot.

9. To finish, I worked two rows of netting without shells, then pulled all the strings together to tie them in one large overhand knot.

KNOW YOUR KNOTS

The knots featured here are some of the most basic, and are the ones used for the projects in this chapter. If you want to expand your knowledge, you can find more information in books devoted to knot craft or on the Internet.

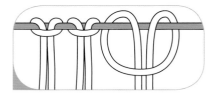

Lark's Head Knot

Use this knot to attach fiber to a base cord on the gourd or through holes drilled around a rim. To make the knot, you begin by folding one length of fiber in half. By passing the two ends through the loop, you get two working strands.

Overhand Knot

This knot is so common you probably thought it didn't have a name. It's the knot you use to tie your shoes and at the end of thread to secure it when sewing by hand. The project Talking Knots (page 118) employs this knot to create the textured effect. First, make a loop, next, bring the end of the strand behind the loop, and then pull it tight.

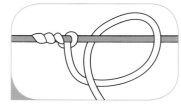

Half Hitch

You can entirely cover a gourd with dense, half-hitch knots. Or, you can work a few rows of half hitch to make a decorative border that also acts as a secure base for beginning other techniques. To make it, you loop the strand around a base cord, and then simply pull it in place.

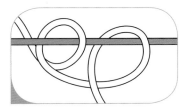

Double Half Hitch

Also known as the clove hitch, the double half hitch is one of the most popular knots employed in macramé. You begin by first knotting a half hitch around a base cord, and then you repeat, using the same working strand.

Square Knot

The Moroccan Bottle (page 127) is a prime example of working the square knot on a gourd. The knot is made in a two-part sequence, with two cords as anchor strands and two cords as working strands. Select two strands as the anchor strands. The two lengths on either side will be the working strands. Pass the left working strand over the anchor strands and under the working strand on the right.

Then pass the right working strand under the anchor strands and out through the loop on the left. Cinch tight. For the second part of the sequence, lay the right working strand over the anchor strands. Pass the left working strand under the anchor strands and through the loop on the right. Cinch tight.

Half Knot

The half knot repeats the first half of the square-knot sequence to create a decorative twist. If you want a twist to the right, always start with the left-hand cord; for a twist to the left, always start with the right-hand cord. Pass the left working strand over the anchor strands and under the

working strand on the right. Then pass the left working strand over the anchor strands and under the right working strand. Pass the right working strand under the anchor strands and out through the loop on the left. Cinch tight, and repeat.

Josephine Knot

Because this purely decorative knot won't support weight or take much tension, use it as an embellishment only. Start with the left strand and loop it over the right strand. Pass the right strand over the end of the left strand, and then

loop it up and under the left strand. Pass the end of the same strand over the other strand, then under itself, and then out through the loop on the right. Cinch, but avoid cinching too tightly or you will distort the shape.

The half hitch is one of the simplest knots to make. Using it creates a dense, textured surface on the gourd. You'll use the end of the base cord as a core for knotting the working strands around it.

Small **GOURD**, cleaned and finished ● Waxed linen **THREAD** in a variety of colors

WHAT YOU DO

1. Cut lengths from the waxed linen thread, each approximately six times the estimated length of the project. Each length will become two working ends. Cut enough lengths of thread to go around slightly less than half the diameter of the gourd at the base cord.

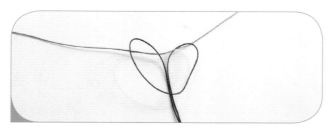

2. Attach the working strands to the base cord *off* the gourd. Using one of the cut threads for the base cord, begin attaching the working strands using the lark's head knot (page 122). Cinch each tight to the base cord.

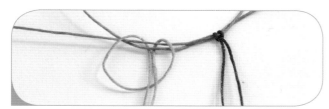

3. After you've attached several working strands, circle the ends of the base cord, and attach the remainder of the working ends over this doubled base cord.

4. Pull the ends of the base cord together.

5. Place the base cord around the top of the gourd, and pull the ends tight to cinch it. For this project, I left the stem on and slipped the base cord over it.

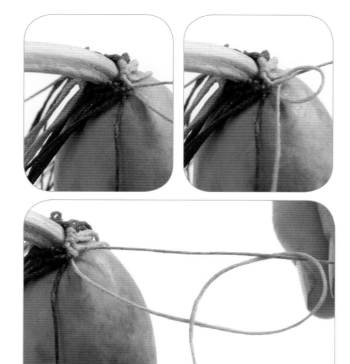

6. One end of the base cord will become the core around which you knot. Gently pull the end out to separate it from the working strands. Pass the first adjacent working strand over and behind the end of the base cord. Then pull the end through the resulting loop, and cinch it tight. This completes a single half hitch (page 122). To make a double half hitch (page 123), repeat, using the same working strand.

7. Continue working around the gourd, always knotting over the base cord with the next adjacent working strand. As the diameter decreases, use single half hitches. As the diameter increases, continue using double half hitches.

8. If you run out of a working strand, or if you want to add a different color, use a lark's head knot to mount the new strand on the core, and continue knotting. If you want to discontinue a color, simply drop the end behind and under the knotting. You can cut the end, or, if you think you might use it later, let it hang behind the knot and then pick it up when you want.

9. The working strands extend from the knotted structure as if they're flowing out of the gourd. If you desire, you can further embellish your design with buttons or beads. Since I wanted to evoke a volcano, I wrapped the stem of the gourd and strung red beads to resemble drops of lava. I finished by mounting the piece on a flat stone.

tip ➔ You can continue knotting all the way around the surface of the gourd, or you can knot in just one area by bringing the core back and forth over the area you selected.

Artist ● **Alfie Davis**

This might look complicated, but the basis of this project is simple square-knot macramé. The constantly challenging shapes of a bottle gourd can bring new and exciting dimensions to this old craft form.

WHAT YOU NEED

Bottle **GOURD**, cut, cleaned, and finished ● Hemp **CORD** ● **T-PINS**

WHAT YOU DO

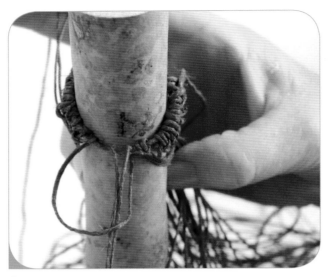

1. Cut each length of cord eight times the estimated length of the project. Each length will become two working strands. Use a length of cord for the base cord and attach it to the gourd, letting its ends hang down. Cut each length just before attaching it to the base cord using the lark's head knot (page 122). Add strands until they loosely surround the neck of the gourd. Make sure the working strands, including the two ends of the base cord, are a multiple of four.

2. Secure the cords by knotting an anchor row. Select one end of the base cord to be the core, then work a single row of double half hitches (page 123) around it. T-pins help hold the knotting in place when you start a project and are helpful to use any time when needed.

3. Begin the square-knot sequence. Select two strands for anchor strands. The two strands on either side will be the working strands. Pass the working strand from the left side *over* the anchor strands and *under* the working strand on the right. Then pass the working strand from the right side *under* the anchor strands and out through the loop created between the left working strand and the anchor strands. Cinch tight.

4. For the second half of the square-knot sequence, lay the right working strand *over* the anchor strands. Pass the left working strand *under* the anchor strands and out through the loop on the right. Cinch tight.

5. Using the next set of four strands, repeat the process until you've tied all the strands to complete the first row. For the second row, use two strands from each of the knots in the first row to begin the knotting. The working strands in the first row become the anchor strands in the second row, and vice versa. It's this alternating from anchor to working strands row after row that creates this solid structure.

6. After working several inches of the square knot, you may want to add variety to the knotting pattern. You can make a chain using the square knot by repeatedly knotting the sequence over the same anchor strands. To create a chain with a twist, use the half knot (page 123) that repeats only the first part of the square-knot sequence. In this project, I always brought the working strand from the left *over* the anchor strands.

7. When the gourd diameter increases, you can add additional strands by attaching them around the existing strands. Just be sure the number of working strands is always a multiple of four. For this gourd, I used double square knot chains and twisted chains to create an open netted effect. For additional interest, I strung beads on the anchor cords as I knotted the chains.

8. To finish off, I repeated the square-knot pattern around the bottom of the gourd, cinching it tighter to the gourd as needed. Once the square knots became very close together, I knotted several rows of half hitches, as I did at the top, to anchor the cords. I then clipped the ends and tucked them under the knotting.

tip ➤ As I was working, I thought a darker background would show the knotting to greater effect. Before beginning the knotting on the rounded part of the gourd, I slipped off the knotted neck, painted the gourd, replaced the knotting, and resumed my work.

KNOTTING

Show off your knot craft. Your biggest decision in making this project will be whether to cover the entire gourd with Josephine knots, or make space for highlighting even fancier knots.

WHAT YOU NEED

GOURD, cut, cleaned, and finished ● Gourd or leather **AWL** ● **CORD**, approximately ¼ inch (6 mm) in diameter ● **T-PINS** ● Waxed linen **THREAD** ● Tapestry **NEEDLE**

WHAT YOU DO

1. Use the awl to make an even number of evenly spaced holes around the rim ½ to ¾ inch (1.3 to 1.9 cm) apart. Determine how many cut lengths of cord you'll need to circle the gourd; each knot begins with a pair of cords. Cut each length of cord eight times the length of the gourd.

2. Use the T-pins to hold the cords in place by placing the T-pins in the holes. Fold the cords in half, draping the folds over the T-pins to give each cord two working ends. Make a loop in the left cord.

3. Bring the right-hand working end under the loop just created, and over the end of the left cord.

4. Bring the working end of the right cord under the upper portion of the left cord.

5. Then bring it over the upper side of the loop, under itself, and over the lower edge of the loop. You can use a small hook made of wire or a crochet hook to pull the end through.

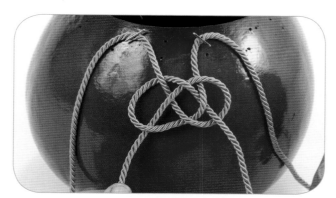

6. Gently pull both ends to tighten the knot. Work a row around the gourd using the remaining cords. When you get to the second row, and all rows following, pair the cords by taking an end from each knot.

7. I decided beforehand that I wanted to work three decorative knots on the sides of the gourd. To accommodate the extra length of cord these knots would take, I cut the cords I would be using for them at least 1 yard (.9 m) longer than the others.

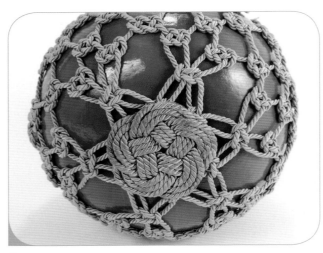

8. After tying all the Josephine knots, combine four ends, and work half hitches (page 122) to cinch the cording around the bottom of the gourd. You can work a fancy knot at the bottom. Or, you can clip the ends of the cords, and cover them with a circle of leather. If you clip the cords, dab each end with white glue to prevent them from fraying before gluing the circle over them.

9. To finish the top, use the waxed linen thread and tapestry needle to stitch the cords to the rim through the holes before removing the T-pins. Make a belt of Josephine knots long enough to fit snug against the rim of the gourd.

10. Stitch the belt to the rim through the holes using waxed linen thread, catching the knotting cords as you go.

tip ——▶ Practice makes perfect in knot craft. Practice the Josephine knot off the gourd following the instructions on page 123 before beginning the project.

Variation

The same project in black

After burnishing the shell of a green banana gourd to a beautiful finish,
you decoratively wrap it in rattan. This simple ornamentation organically
complements the elegant lines of the gourd.

WHAT YOU NEED

Banana **GOURD** ● Sanding **SPONGES** in 180-, 500-, and 1000-grit ● **BONE** folder, polished stone, or table **KNIFE** ● 20 feet (6.1 m) of 3.5 mm **RATTAN** cane ● Craft **KNIFE** with sharp blade ● Sharp **SCISSORS**

WHAT YOU DO

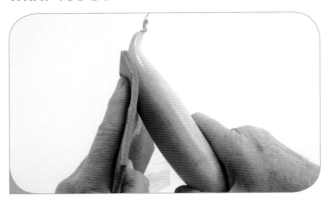

1. Make sure the green-scraped gourd you select is free from mold markings. Use the sanding sponges to progressively wet sand the shell to enhance its natural beauty and give it depth. Start with the 180-grit sponge, then the 500-grit, and finish with the 1000-grit.

2. Use the bone folder, smooth stone, or the backside of a table knife to burnish the surface by vigorously rubbing it over the gourd's shell. The more you burnish, the higher the sheen.

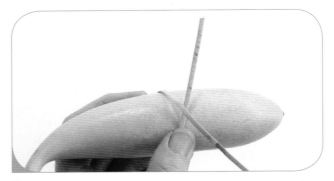

3. Make a loop of cane around the gourd, bringing the long end around the vertical shorter end.

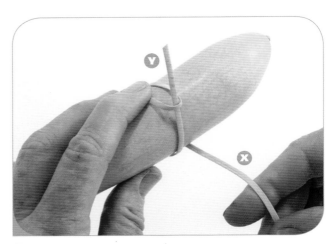

4. Bring the long end X around the vertical short end Y and then back around the gourd. Then bring the strand up and to the front of the gourd.

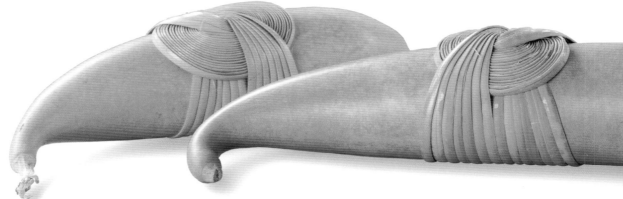

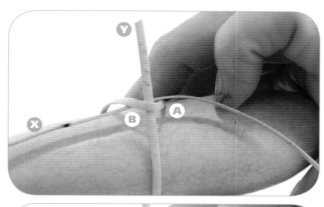

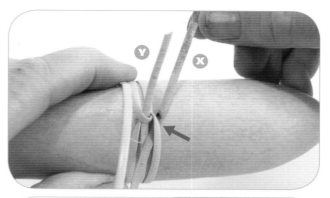

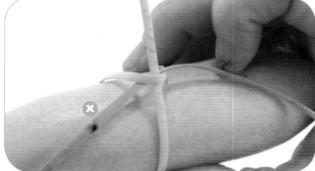

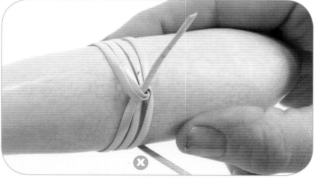

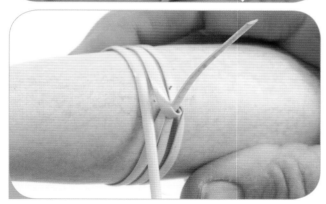

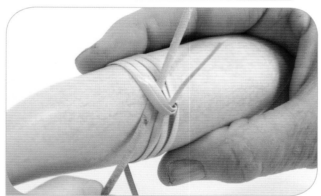

5. Slip end X around the vertical short end Y, over A, and under B. Bring X to the front of the gourd, then down and around the gourd to the knot on top. Pull snug.

6. Bring X around Y and under the loop at the arrow, following the first course. Pull the strand snug, and bring X around the top of the gourd again. Continue this weaving pattern until you complete four to five courses.

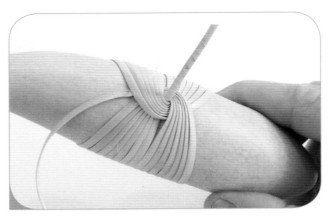

7. This shows five completed courses. You could trim the ends and finish here, but there is a second step to this knot that is really awesome.

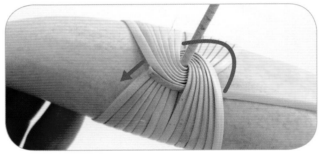

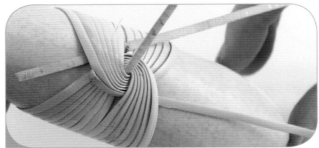

8. Bring the strand around and back through the opening in the knot and pull snug. Then bring the strand around and through the opening of the knot on the opposite side and pull it snug.

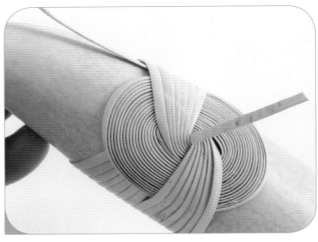

9. Continue around and around the center of the knot as often as desired or until you run out of room in the opening of the knot. Pull the end as snug as possible, and wedge it under the knot.

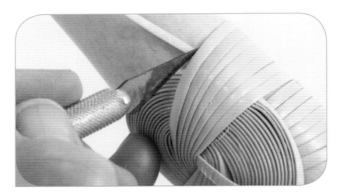

10. Use the craft knife with a sharp blade to trim the end to hide it.

11. Trim the vertical strand as close as possible to the knot to hide the end.

12. To complete the project, I mounted it vertically in the end of another gourd using a small wooden dowel set in holes drilled in both gourds, which I glued in place.

Artist ● **Flo Hoppe**

Artist ● **Flo Hoppe**

Artist ● **Marjorie Albright**

CHAPTER 8

FELTING AND CROCHET

The gourd was a highly regarded vessel in all cultures, and any adaptation that extended its working years or made it easier to use was a valuable discovery. Since people made baskets and employed netting techniques for utilitarian purposes, it's easy to see how they could translate those techniques for use on a gourd.

However, many fiber techniques, such as crochet, knitting, and felting, never made the evolutionary leap to traditional use on gourds—even if you argue that knitting and crochet are a form of knotless netting. Perhaps people more closely identified these techniques with making fabric and clothing than with vessels. Whatever the reason, these imposed cultural restrictions no longer apply. Today in the world of gourds, you can use these techniques with exciting results.

Artists have been experimenting with crochet, knitting, and felting on gourds to create new forms. If we were able to go back in time and bring these objects to our ancestors, they might not recognize the application of these techniques on gourds. What they would recognize, however, is man's timeless need to try new ways of satisfying the creative spirit.

Felting

Felting is a process of turning wool into a solid yet flexible piece of fabric. Although it's an ancient fiber technique, probably dating from Neolithic times, felting has recently made a dramatic resurgence in the craft world. Wool is the primary ingredient in felt making, but you can integrate other fibers into the work during the felting process to create unique surfaces and designs.

You may have created a felted object yourself if you've accidentally put a wool garment into a washer and dryer by mistake. Wetting and pressing wool fibers together with hot soapy water causes the individual fibers to swell and the scales on their surfaces to open up. As the fibers rub together and shrink, the opened scales grab onto each other and cause the fibers to interlock.

The traditional method of creating felt is to begin with carded fleece that has the strands lying in one direction. After crisscrossing several layers of fleece on top of each other, you pat the mass of fleece with hot soapy water to begin forming it into a mat or bat. As you continue to massage the piece with increasing pressure, the fibers interlock and the mat becomes firmer.

You can follow the same process for covering a gourd in felt by wrapping it in multiple layers of fleece as you pat and massage the mat to shape it around the gourd. Try to select a gourd with a firm shell that will withstand the pressure you apply when felting. The shell should not be slick or shiny. If it is, you can sand the shell with a coarse-grit sandpaper to allow the fleece to adhere better during the felting process.

To hold the fleece securely to the shape of the gourd, you wrap it with string, yarn, or even thread, before wetting it. You can use decorative yarns that are not wool, since they will be held in place by the wool fibers as they begin to interlace and shrink. After the gourd and felt are dry, you can loosen bits of the decorative yarn for accent. Another easy design element is to use different colors of wool fleece as you layer it, which will create interesting patterns in the finished felt.

Crochet

Crochet creates a structure of interlocking loops using a hook that works a continuous strand of fiber. People have used it for hundreds of years to make clothing or utilitarian household objects, such as bags and blankets. They also used it as a way to decorate cloth, such as edging on collars or household items.

Artists familiar with crochet techniques have joined these skills with their love of gourds to create many distinctive pieces. The most popular use is to add a top to a cut gourd, either for decorating the rim or creating a purse you can cinch closed. You can use any type of material for your crochet, from natural wool to synthetics, from string to wire.

FUZZY

Designer ● **Rebecca Black**

Artist Rebecca Black shows another way to use crochet on a gourd. After drilling holes through the shell, she used fuzzy yarn to crochet through the holes to create the rim treatment. She planned a path along the gourd and drilled holes along it. She crocheted a fuzzy strip the length of the path and attached it to the gourd by stitching through the holes as you would when couching in chapter 3. Rebecca finished the inside of the gourd with decoupage, then added crystals to embellish the design.

Artist ● **Ginger Summit**

Artist ● **Ginny Nordling**

When working crochet on a gourd, you first need to establish a way to anchor the yarn or threads to the gourd. The two most common ways to do this are: drilling holes in the shell that are large enough for the crochet hook to pass through, and stitching a row of yarn or thread around the gourd through holes you've drilled in the shell. In the latter method, you can use either a running stitch or overhand stitch. Stitching three or four single crochet stitches into each hole will create a pretty "V" effect.

Stitching a row of three single crochet stitches into each hole drilled through the rim of the gourd also provides an elegant transition to crochet, knitting, or looping. Another way to begin is to simply crochet a chain or a few rows of pattern in the round, then slip this crocheted circle over the neck of the gourd. Some crafters choose to bypass crocheting on the gourd altogether by completing a crocheted piece first before attaching it to the gourd with stitches taken through holes drilled in the shell.

Artist ● **Kathleen Storey**

FUN FELT FUN FELT FUN FELT FUN FELT FUN FELT FUN FELT
FUN FELT **FUN FELT** FUN FELT FUN FELT FUN FELT FUN FEL
FUN FELT FUN FELT FUN FELT FUN FELT FUN FELT FUN

The technique of felting meets gourd craft creates this thoroughly modern art object. As you experiment with the technique, try covering an entire gourd or just portions of one with felted fleece.

WHAT YOU NEED

GOURD, cut, cleaned, and finished ● Coarse-grit **SANDPAPER** ● Wool **FLEECE** ● **YARN, THREAD**, or **ROVING**
● Hot **WATER** ● **SOAP** flakes, *not* detergent ● Surgical **GLOVES** ● Plastic bag ● Hair **DRYER** *(optional)* ●
BEADS, yarn, or other decorative elements *(optional)*

WHAT YOU DO

1. Use the coarse-grit sandpaper to sand the surface of the gourd to make the fleece adhere better.

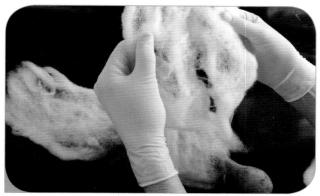

2. If the fleece has not been carded, arrange small pieces with all the fibers lying in the same direction.

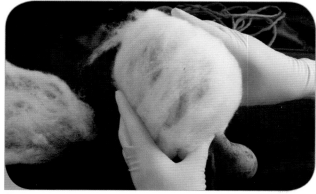

3. Wrap the pieces of fleece around the surface of the gourd. Add additional layers, laying each at right angles to the layer before. Evenly cover the gourd, filling in any gaps with small pieces of additional fleece.

4. Wrap the yarn, thread, or roving around the gourd to keep the fleece in place.

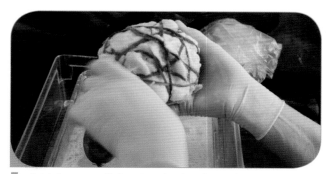

5. Add the soap flakes to a basin of very hot water, adding enough to make a thin gel. Sprinkle the soapy water on the fleece, and gently squeeze until you've saturated all the layers. Wear the surgical gloves to protect your hands.

6. Slip the plastic bag over the gourd, tightly securing it at the neck. Start with a gentle massage, then gradually increase the pressure and force of rubbing. Continue rubbing vigorously until the felt is solid and has adhered to the gourd's surface.

7. Remove the plastic bag, and rinse the gourd to remove the soapy water. Handle the gourd gently. If you find areas where the fleece feels loose, add soapy water and rub to felt the fleece, then rinse. Allow the gourd to dry. Embellish the gourd, if desired, using beads, yarns, or other decorative elements.

tip ——▶ Use a hair dryer to provide additional heat to the felting process and to hasten drying.

ANCIENT MEMORY

Artist ● **Ginger Summit**

We know that traditionally felting was not a fiber technique used on gourds. However, when you see this object you can hardly believe it. This is an example of applying a new technique to make an object look like an ancient artifact. For this project, I applied a dark stain to the gourd and used a dark fleece for the felting. I used dark braided cording for wrapping the fleece in a random pattern. A large tassel complements the braiding and embellishes the design for a perfect finish.

Artist ● **Jan Banta Briseno**

Artist ● **Jill Walker**

About the Authors

In 1990 Ginger Summit became intrigued with the idea of decorating gourds. However, in pursuing this interest, she found that very little had been written about the subject and that instructional books were few and far between. What began as a craft interest quickly became a passion as she discovered unusual uses of gourds in marketplaces and museums around the world. Extensive contact with craftspeople and artists in this country revealed a vital interest in gourds as a new medium for expression. As a retired teacher, Ginger wanted to share this newfound knowledge with others, hoping to provide the long needed resources by writing books and articles on gourds.

Jim Widess has been providing classes on gourd craft and selling gourds and gourd craft supplies since 1969. He's the owner of The Caning Shop (www.caning.com), in Berkeley, California, and co-authored *The Caner's Handbook* (Lark Books, 1991), the definitive book on all aspects of woven chair seat repair. As a photographer, he has a zeal for visual instructions for crafts. Jim photographed all the how-to pictures in this book.

Other books by Ginger Summit and Jim Widess:
Complete Book of Gourd Craft
ISBN 978-1887374552

Complete Book of Gourd Carving
ISBN 978-1402748721

Making Gourd Dolls & Spirit Figures
ISBN 978-1402732201

Making Gourd Musical Instruments
ISBN 978-1402745034

Also by Ginger Summit:
Gourds in Your Garden
ISBN 978-0965869157

The Weekend Crafter: Gourd Crafts
ISBN 978-1579901523

Also by Jim Widess:
Gourd Pyrography
ISBN 978-1402745027

The Complete Guide to Chair Caning
ISBN 978-1579906139

Plaited Basketry with Birch Bark
ISBN 978-1402748097

Acknowledgments

We wish to thank Cindy Lee, Diane Calderwood, Linda Pietz, Marjorie Albright, and Susie Billingsley for providing several of the projects in this volume. We are indebted to the hundreds of gourd artists, those represented here and those who aren't because of space limitations, who contributed photos, shared ideas and techniques, and encouraged us to undertake this fascinating study of the uses of fibers with gourds. We hope the reader not only learns new methods but also brings new materials and techniques to the field.

Caution Advisory: Gourds are in the squash family and have hard, woody shells. They have been grown for use as containers, and resonators for musical instruments, as well as a source for high fat content seeds for animals for millennia. When crafting gourds, the artist should be mindful of mold spores and the dust created by drilling and cutting. Some folks are very allergic to gourd dust. We encourage the wearing of a respirator when cleaning, cutting, or drilling into gourds. Likewise, eye protection should be worn when engaging in any activity which creates gourd dust or small pieces of gourds. Tools, such as saws, awls, drills, and knives are sharp and can cause pain and injury. We advise using care and common sense, as well as staying alert, when using any tool.

The authors always enjoy hearing from you and sharing your joy of gourds and weaving. Please contact them at: jimandginger@caning.com.

GALLERY

Artist ● **Browning House**

Index